Quality Connections

Transforming Schools Through Total Quality Management

Randy Schenkat

Association for Supervision and Curriculum Development
Alexandria, Virginia

About the Author

Randy Schenkat is the Director of the Winona Council of Quality in Winona, Minnesota. He has twenty years of experience as an educator at all levels with a principal focus on staff development and organizational change in meeting needs of hard-to-teach students. Address correspondence to Randy Schenkat, 1419 Conrad Dr., Winona, MN 55987; phone, (507) 452-7168.

Printed in the United States of America. Typeset on Xerox™ Ventura Publisher 4.1.

Association for Supervision and Curriculum Development
1250 N. Pitt Street   Alexandria, VA 22314-1453
Telephone (703) 549-9110   FAX (703) 549-3891

Ronald S. Brandt, *Executive Editor*
Nancy Modrak, *Managing Editor, Books*
Carolyn R. Pool, *Associate Editor*
Jennifer Beun, *Assistant Editor*
Gary Bloom, *Manager, Design and Production Services*
Karen Monaco, *Senior Designer*
Keith Demmons, *Designer*
Stephanie Kenworthy, *Assistant Manager, Production Services*
Valerie Sprague, *Desktop Publisher*

Price: $13.95
ASCD Stock No.: 611-93013
ISBN: 0-87120-203-4

Library of Congress Cataloging-in-Publication Data

Schenkat, Randy.
    Quality connections : transforming schools through Total Quality
  Management / Randy Schenkat.
      p.   cm.
    Includes bibliographical references.
    ISBN 0-87120-203-4
    1. School management and organization—United States. 2. Total
  quality management—United States. 3. School improvement programs—
  United States. 4. Educational leadership—United States.
  I. Title.
  LB2805.S34   1993
  371.2'00973—dc20   93-18529
                                              CIP

Quality Connections: Transforming Schools Through Total Quality Management

Acknowledgments

This book took a different path. I am in debt to Ron Brandt for recognizing and supporting that path.

Much of the passionate belief I hope the book conveys about the importance of leadership and the belief in the "quality" style of leadership to lead us out of the crisis has come from my interaction with two leaders who truly "walk the talk"—Dan Rukavina, Co-CEO of EMD, Inc. of Winona, Minnesota, and David Romstad, Superintendent of Parkview District, Orfordville, Wisconsin.

The emerging vision of community that has a critical role for education has sustained me in the couple of years this book has been fermenting. My fellow travelers in the Winona Council for Quality have provided much sustenance.

As I reflect on my parents' modeling in their conduct of business, I am aware of their sense of quality and their influence. My wife, Jeanne, has also understood and has supported the path of the book. In addition, I acknowledge the fortuitous connection in working with Phyllis Albertz to communicate the many abstractions in this book.

Finally, I would like to acknowledge Carolyn Pool, ASCD associate editor, for her able skills and fine sense of the intent in polishing the book.

RANDY SCHENKAT
Winona, Minnesota

Preface

Looking at things from a business perspective is second nature to me. I have experienced all facets of running a family-owned manufacturing and retail business; and I earned an undergraduate degree in business administration before entering education more than two decades ago. I entered the profession as a school psychologist steeped in Reger's (1965, 1970) tradition as an internal consultant. This role has paralleled W. Edwards Deming's notion of an in-house leader in statistical methodology.

I also have held positions as a learning disabilities teacher, special education administrator, and learning disabilities professor before beginning work as a project director in a federally funded project to weave mainstreaming competencies into a preservice teacher education program. This project took a much different tack from that of 400 other projects of this type throughout the United States. At the time, I was unaware that we were applying many of Deming's ideas—first to a teacher education program and then to an entire liberal arts college.

In this teacher education project, we linked our efforts to Peters and Waterman's *In Search of Excellence* (1982). The title of our book, *It Stands to Reason: The Rationale and Implementation of a Development Based, Liberal Arts Oriented, Teacher-Education Program* (Schenkat, Battaglini, and Rosen 1985), provides a sense of the issues considered. Key among these was our concern that faculty know the extended process of student cognitive development. This primary interest in cognitive development has spread into work in both child and adult cognitive development (Sambs and Schenkat 1990; Morehouse, Schenkat, and Battaglini 1991).

Systems optimization offers many advances in teacher education preparation. It also offers a new way of looking at K–12 schools' failure with hard-to-teach students (at-risk learners). As early as 1980, we conducted projects funded from the U.S. Department of Education, Office of Special Education, to ameliorate the failure of learners with mild disabilities. These projects focused on getting systems to work better together.

We found that the missing piece in systems change in the K–12 environment was a passionate commitment by leaders to this form of improvement. Having struggled throughout the decade of the '80s with projects that attempted systems change without the solid support of leadership, I came to believe that Deming's ideas, which focused to such a great extent on leadership, seemed to be the missing ingredient.

As I was becoming aware of Deming by readings in the late 1980s, I also was becoming aware of how the "quality movement" was taking hold in the state of Minnesota, particularly in Winona. Over the past two years, I have become immersed in Total Quality Management (TQM), particularly from a Deming perspective. As a result of my active role in our informal Winona Council for Quality, I was asked to become the first staff person for this organization when we formally incorporated in 1992. The Council seeks to support the application of TQM throughout the community so that all sectors—business, government, and education—work as a holistic system.

I took a risk in using the acronym TQM. It becomes a lighting rod and is subject to the same type of semantic debate as that surrounding other educational acronyms, such as OBE (outcome-based education). I'm still reading of debate concerning OBE as I write these last words for the book. Moreover, I'm aware that Deming doesn't espouse the use of TQM as a phrase. It is my hope that the book conveys the sense and urgency of our challenge and offers many facets to attend to in developing the types of educational futures we need. From my sense of operationalizing terms, I see TQM as synchronizing these many facets into a holistic or *total* approach to change, guided by Deming's quality principles. I hope this sense of *urgency* and *possibility* creates a belief that there are more productive things to do than engage in semantic debates over labels of movements.

Introduction:
The Quality Connection

Total Quality Management (TQM), the synchronization of quality principles across an organization, holds many answers to the challenges educators face. It helps us see our problems as difficulties within systems and not with people. In our educational systems, teachers are often held prisoners in intellectually void cells; true learning communities are rare. The processes used in day-to-day instruction, such as rote learning and performance-derived self-concepts, fall far short of the state of the art of effective teaching. Systemic barriers continue to rob teachers of their pride in workmanship; and the authoritarian, hierarchical processes used by leadership are contrary to TQM practices.

TQM also helps us see solutions in a comprehensive, big picture. It allows us to make *connections* with many of the contemporary findings regarding educational excellence. Constancy of purpose allows school districts or local schools to come up with timelines for solutions and thus to realistically allow for meaningful change. Also, TQM solutions can be shared with leaders from all sectors of the community and conveyed to all community members. The solutions are understandable.

Understanding and Embracing
Total Quality Management

It is my intent to present TQM principles in a format that makes TQM accessible to educational leaders. The book is based heavily on the work of W. Edwards Deming and many of his key ideas, including his insistence that:

- Over 90 percent of the problems are with systems.
- Organizations need a constancy of purpose.
- A profound knowledge of systems, variation, knowledge, and psychology must guide an organization.
- Leadership will get us out of the crisis.

Another important source of the ideas in this book is the Malcolm Baldrige Award criteria. The popular criteria can serve as guideposts for achieving quality in any organization, including schools.

The Framework for This Book

Chapter 1 introduces the work of W. Edwards Deming and relates his philosophy to critical contemporary education issues, such as self-concept, intrinsic motivation, cooperative learning, problem solving, systems thinking, dealing with ambiguity, and conceptual change. By linking Deming to contemporary educational issues, I point out two challenges that TQM brings to educators. First, we face the significant changes that any organization undergoes as it switches from a customary management style to TQM. Second, using a business metaphor, we have to completely retool "mass production" education to a custom-crafting of individual "products." This calls for a new "core technology."

Chapter 2 deals with overcoming educators' resistance to a business model—for example, using such business terms as *product, customer, supplier, worker, manager,* and even *system.* On the other hand, the chapter notes the similarity between Deming's TQM philosophy and the deep-seated beliefs of most teachers. I describe the changing world economic order and education's critical role in the standard of living. This chapter discusses four reasons for supporting TQM:

• Business educational needs are closely related to a liberal education.
• There is a groundswell of endorsement for TQM in the community.
• Unions are also endorsing TQM.
• TQM helps dignify and unite current educational changes.

Chapter 3 introduces the Malcolm Baldrige National Quality Award and describes its impact on business in the United States. The Baldrige Award criteria are used in the remainder of the book as concrete ways to apply Deming's thinking to schools. The Baldrige Award is similar to a set of developmental criteria that chronicle the growth of an individual. I have emphasized the leader's role in fostering this development (using the Baldrige criterion, "Leadership").

Chapter 4 examines the new educational "product," or outcome, and points out an almost timeless standard of good education. The real issue isn't coming to clarity on the educational outcome, but rather in understanding why the processes of education have failed us. Educational processes need to be much more interdependent, with the teacher synchronization necessary to foster self-regulated learners. Parents have a role as "suppliers" in learning readiness. The Baldrige criterion discussed here is "Quality Assurance of Products and Services."

Chapter 5 highlights the human resource development needs in meeting the national education goals. Teacher job skills are the foundation to common TQM practices of awareness of TQM, quality tools, and group process skills. Evidence leads me to suggest that (1) few teachers have learned content beyond facts, (2) conceptual paradigms affect teacher performance, and (3) K–12 schools work poorly as learning organizations for teachers. In Deming terminology, we do not possess the profound knowledge that undergirds our core technologies. Helpful strategies to enhance teacher development are included in the Baldrige criterion, "Human Resources Development and Management."

Chapter 6 describes the remaining Baldrige criteria: "Customer Focus and Satisfaction," the "Strategic Quality Plan," "Information and Analysis," and "Quality and Operational Results." These criteria are followed by their educational implications. I suggest being guided by a realization that what the student (customer) wants in the short run is not necessarily of long-term value. Also, various parenting styles may be incompatible with the fostering of self-regulated learners. The discussion of *Strategic Quality Planning* points to the importance of designing in quality over an extended time frame. The section on *Information and Analysis* gives examples of benchmarking and the value of aggregating and disaggregating data. An examination of *Quality and Operational Results* shows that quality is not caused by serendipity. For instance, much of what we attribute to education could be coincidental, for children who have educationally stimulating home environments. And educators would be well advised to accept that quality will be less expensive in the long run.

Chapter 7 presents and explains a matrix that encompasses three time frames: the start-up, operation, and sustenance of a TQM program in a school district. The matrix illustrates types of activities that might be undertaken in the seven Baldrige criteria areas.

The conclusion describes the quality journey in terms of living in a new environment, "the high country of the mind," and relates TQM "profound knowledge" to educational outcomes.

Purposes of the Book

It is my hope that educators will interact with the thoughts throughout this book, with the following purposes:

• To understand TQM, primarily through the lens of W. Edwards Deming and the Baldrige Award criteria.

• To see parallels of TQM to educational transformation, while noting the rigor that TQM can add to our education efforts.

• To develop a personal capacity to interact with confidence with business and community leaders.

• To discriminate between TQM applications that hold promise and those that could be pitfalls.

• To envision a new era of education based on economic trends that TQM's application can foster, providing an optimistic future for American education.

• To convey the power of TQM to internal and external stakeholders, gain allies, and begin to shape a TQM plan for your district—designing in quality, reallocating resources, and coalescing educators' sentiments about TQM's use.

1

The Deming Paradigm and Conceptual Change

Public education in the United States is at a crossroads. We can become a centerpiece of American life in the age of intellectual capital, or we can dwindle into a woefully underfunded, irrelevant enterprise. Total Quality Management (TQM) and, especially, the thinking and work of W. Edwards Deming can be useful to American education. The Deming method is based on leadership through understanding, continuous improvement through personal growth and education, constancy of purpose, and elimination of barriers to self-fulfillment. It is also based on a system of profound knowledge, as Deming terms it, built on understanding of theories of systems, variation, knowledge, and psychology.

Deming's approach provides a means for job satisfaction and self-fulfillment, as leaders strive to understand and mitigate the forces of destruction that cause humiliation, fear, defensiveness, and a dependence on extrinsic motivation. In the TQM process, practices such as judging and ranking employees are stopped. TQM seeks to restore intrinsic motivation, self-esteem, dignity, cooperation, curiosity, and joy in learning. This is what schools and learning should be about for both students and teachers.

There are quality challenges for American education today. The TQM route offers a direction in answering many educational dilemmas. For instance, it is possible to have caring, well-intended teachers giving their all and yet not attaining the educational results needed. For the most part, problems aren't with individuals, but rather with systems; and people often do not notice the systems. This is Deming's most important point: 90 percent of problems with quality are problems with systems, not with people. Sarason (1990) makes this point concerning the American educational enterprise:

If I intended to convey anything, it is that the traditional model of classroom organization, as well as that of the school and school system, creates rather than dilutes problems that adversely affect or greatly constrict the productivity of all participants in the educational arena. What we have now is not working to anyone's satisfaction (p. 95).

This acknowledgment that problems are in the system is clearly illustrated by Fullan's (1991) description of the typical classroom:

The picture is one of limited development of technical culture: teachers are uncertain about how to influence students, especially about noncognitive goals, and even about whether they are having an influence; they experience students as individuals in specific circumstances who, taken as a classroom of individuals, are being influenced by multiple and differing forces for which generalizations are not possible; teaching decisions are often made on pragmatic trial-and-error grounds with little chance for reflection or thinking through the rationale; teachers must deal with constant and daily disruptions, within the classroom in managing discipline and interpersonal conflicts, and from outside the classroom in collecting money for school events, making announcements, dealing with the principal, parent, central office staff, etc.; they must get through the daily grind; the rewards are having a few good days, covering the curriculum, getting a lesson across, having an impact on one or two individual students (success stories); they constantly feel the critical shortage of time (p. 33).

In this description of classrooms, Fullan points to several systems problems: lack of time, constant disruptions, lack of reward or a sense of influence, and a press for curriculum coverage. TQM helps to ensure that all aspects of the system work in harmony to achieve the primary purpose of the system: learning. Schools have the same characteristics as most organizations, with many factors that reduce or suboptimize the goal attainment.

Deming's (1986) fourteen points for quality management (Figure 1.1) are becoming well known. Since 1980, with the airing of the National Broadcasting Corporation's TV documentary *If Japan Can, Why Can't We?* Deming has had a dramatic impact on American business. His story is chronicled in many sources (Walton 1991); and within the past year, countless articles have made suggestions for the application of the fourteen points to education.

It is hard to argue that constancy of purpose, instituting on-the-job training, continuous improvement, and the other eleven points shouldn't be applied to schools. But how do we go about integrating TQM with other educational initiatives, such as performance assessment, outcome-based education, at-risk programming, constructivism, and whole language? The implementation of any of these initiatives can seem overwhelming in its own right. The question is not whether to

FIGURE 1.1
Deming's Fourteen Points:
A Theory for Management Transformation

1. Create constancy of purpose toward improvement of product and service, with the aim to become competitive and to stay in business, and to provide jobs.

2. Adopt the new philosophy. We are in a new economic age. Western management must awaken to the challenge, must learn their responsibilities, and take on leadership for change.

3. Cease dependence on inspection to achieve quality. Eliminate the need for inspection on a mass basis by building quality into the product in the first place.

4. End the practice of awarding business on the basis of price tag. Instead, minimize total cost. Move toward a single supplier for any one item, on a long-term relationship of loyalty and trust.

5. Improve constantly and forever the system of production and service, to improve quality and productivity, and thus constantly decrease costs.

6. Institute training on the job.

7. Institute leadership (see point 12). The aim of supervision should be to help people and machines and gadgets to do a better job. Supervision of management is in need of overhaul, as well as supervision of production workers.

8. Drive out fear, so that everyone may work effectively for the company.

9. Break down barriers between departments. People in research, design, sales, and production must work as a team, to foresee problems of production and in use that may be encountered with the product or service.

10. Eliminate slogans, exhortations, and numerical targets for the work force asking for zero defects and new levels of productivity.

11a. Eliminate work standards (quotas) on the factory floor. Substitute leadership.

b. Eliminate management by objective. Eliminate management by numbers, numerical goals. Substitute leadership.

12a. Remove barriers that rob the hourly worker of his right to pride of workmanship. The responsibility of supervisors must be changed from sheer numbers to quality.

b. Remove barriers that rob people in management and in engineering of their right to pride of workmanship. This means, *inter alia*, abolishment of the annual or merit rating and of management by objective .

13. Institute a vigorous program of education and self-improvement.

14. Put everyone in the company to work to accomplish the transformation. The transformation is everybody's job.

Source: Deming, W.E. (1986). *Out of the Crisis.* Cambridge, Mass.: MIT Center for Advanced Engineering Study.

---

implement TQM *or* an innovation such as performance-based assessment. In fact, the TQM process *enhances* the probability of success of proven innovative strategies. I have seen an extensively conceived school transformation project embodying all of these initiatives sputter because it failed to attend to necessary supporting concepts of TQM (Sambs and Schenkat 1990).

The approach I have chosen presents Deming beyond the framework of the common list of the fourteen points. The Deming approach is a congruent set of assumptions, beliefs, attitudes, and practices that is truly a paradigm shift, in the terminology popularized by futurist Joel Barker (1990). Deming has changed the rules of how the organization plays the game by constructing a new set of shared assumptions. TQM is an integrated, holistic world view or a paradigm that is much out of sync with the actions of our society at large and, especially, with American education today. We need to build and support an environment that consistently affirms, supports, and enacts this TQM paradigm.

When I first saw Deming's fourteen points related to education in an article by Jacob Stampen (1987), I immediately saw application. But I did not see Deming's points as a total system of thought calling for a many-faceted paradigm shift based on a system of profound knowledge of theories of systems, variation, knowledge, and psychology. My struggle with Deming's thoughts—finally seeing them as a significant paradigm change—has given me much greater insight into its value for educators. I see his thinking as representative of the deeper understandings that will be needed by educators. These understandings will be needed first by *educational leaders* as they set the conditions for schools to operate in new paradigms.

This struggle has made me realize that many of the educational writings about Deming and his fourteen points were missing some critical deep links that could assist in transforming education. I began to see some of the similarities between the types of thinking that all employees need to apply in TQM organizations and the thinking and paradigms being requested of high school graduates. One specific set of student outcomes is offered by the National Governors' Association (Cohen 1988):

> [Students need] a substantial knowledge base, as well as higher order cognitive skills. Such skills include: the ability to communicate complex ideas, to analyze and solve complex problems, to identify order and find direction in an ambiguous environment, and to think and reason abstractly. Because workers in the future will experience rapid change . . . students also will be required to develop the capacity to learn new skills and tasks quickly. This will require a thorough understanding of the subject matter and an ability to apply this knowledge in creative and imaginative ways, novel contexts, and in collaboration with others (p. 3).

If we fail to see what is implied in this NGA request for the well-educated graduate and try to apply Deming's fourteen points superficially, we could do more damage than good. For instance, it is quite easy to apply statistical process control to mastery scores on the low-level, multiple-choice items used to assess progress in language arts. However, this may only get us better at bad practice. TQM will do double duty for us as educators by guiding the school organizational transformation and by providing psychological and philosophical insights that parallel outcomes of significance for K–12 students.

In this book, rather than go over Deming's fourteen points, I discuss twelve themes—six task and six individual considerations that underlie workplace and school settings (see Figure 1.2).

Using these themes, I contrast the different assumptions underlying customary and transformed settings both in the workplace and in school. This new way of looking at Deming's fourteen points should provide a means to promote understanding and communication among school leaders, school staff, business leaders, company employees, and community members in general. In addition, this view of the two settings clearly indicates much-needed changes in learning outcomes if students are to succeed in a transformed work setting.

Task Issues of Quality Management

Seen through the theme of task issues (the way work is thought of and done), TQM thinking differs from common management practice in several dimensions: the nature of problems, motivation for the task, time frames, the nature of solutions, human capacities used, and the assessment of results. Figure 1.3 shows task issues, the customary management approach to these issues, and a management approach transformed by TQM.

The Nature of the Problem

Contemporary thinking blames people, regulations, and home situations and usually sees problems in isolation, without connections. Deming believes that fully 85–95 percent of all problems are caused by the system. Yesterday's solutions can be seen as today's problems. Also, Deming asserts that all the alleged impediments rolled together make a small bundle compared with the problems that U.S. management has created for itself by such practices as job hopping, emphasis on short-term profits, and management by fear.

FIGURE 1.2

Twelve Themes That Underlie TQM in Workplace and School Settings

Task Issues

Nature of the Problem

Motivation for the Task

Time Frames

Nature of Solutions

Human Capacities Used

Assessing Results

Individual Issues

Self as Learner

Learning from Peers/Experts

View of Self as Person

Success, Challenge, and Failure

Change/Uncertainty

Need for Security

FIGURE 1.3

Tasks in the Workplace

The Task	Customary Practice	Transformed Practice
Nature of the Problem	Blame people, regulations, and the situation	90% is in the system
Motivation for Task	Perform for pay, incentives	People want to do good job; pride in work
Time Frames	Quarterly reporting	Constancy of purpose, 5–10 years to transform
Nature of Solutions	Please the boss; keep answers simple	Seeking root causes, complexity, and understanding
Human Capacities Used	Control, one-upmanship, discussion	Teams responsible, flow of dialogue with assumptions suspended
Assessing Results	Plan and do with little reflection	Plan, Do, Study, Act (PDSA) as a continuous cycle

Motivation for the Task

In common practice, managers believe that employees are motivated by merit ratings and performance evaluations—that people have to be *enticed* into high performance with rewards or punished for low productivity by probations, demotions, layoffs, and so forth. In the transformed setting, we believe that people intrinsically *want* to do a good job. They take a great deal of pride in workmanship. According to Deming, goals, slogans, performance pay, and incentives actually destroy motivation for doing good work.

Time Frames

It is common for quarterly reports to drive American business because there is a continual monitoring of short-term profits. In the new thinking, we realize that there is a tremendous amount of work involved in making the quality transformation. People need constancy of purpose. Leaders must understand that transformation in companies takes from five to ten years. Change must be thought of in longer time frames. Activity cannot be measured by quarterly performance reports.

The Nature of Solutions

Today, a solution often is quickly derived, with perhaps only one idea generated. There is a tendency to keep things simple, to depend on authority: *What does the boss want?* Experts are needed to plan how to implement ideas. In a transformed setting, solutions come from deep understanding and a search for root causes. There is no substitution for knowledge in seeking solutions. We need more complexity—more relationships, more sources of information, more angles, and more direction in ambiguous environments. We must generate multiple ideas and implement the idea most likely to improve the situation.

Human Capacities Used

Customary practice in the workplace includes one-upmanship, with control and a structured chain of command. Often, task demands call for quick answers by individuals who have difficulty making judgments. In the new work setting, each person has ownership and commitment and shares responsibility in a team. There should be a free flow of dialogue with assumptions suspended, a high degree of collegial regard, and attention to task and personal needs.

Assessing Results

In common practice, we plan and do and go on. There is little reflecting on results; the busy pace just keeps people moving on to the next task that needs planning and doing. In contrast, Deming (1992) identifies the Plan, Do, Study, Act (PDSA) cycle (formerly called the PDCA cycle; Deming substituted "study" for "check"). Workers study results of the task to guide action in a continuous improvement cycle. The PDSA cycle is very much like those cycles taught in education methods courses, which stress planning, teaching, evaluating, and reteaching. It is also like the scientific method, which involves making hypotheses, testing, analyzing, and drawing conclusions.

Individual Issues in Quality Management

Another way of understanding Deming is to consider the foundation of the successful individual in a TQM organization. Because Deming is a strong proponent of education/training and an organizational learning culture, his thinking differs from common management practice regarding the individual person. These issues include the self as learner; learning from peers/experts; view of self as a person; success, challenge, and failure; change and uncertainty; and security. Figure 1.4 presents individual issues at the workplace, the common management approach to these issues, and a management approach transformed by TQM.

Self as Learner

How do people at the workplace view themselves as learners and as part of systems? Many people do not recognize ongoing processes at work; they do not look beyond their own niche. In addition, many workers spend their time figuring out what the boss wants. They do not have confidence in their own capacities. In a transformed workplace, the

FIGURE 1.4

The Individual in the Workplace

The Individual	Customary Practice	Transformed Practice
Self as Learner	Challenge seeing process, lacks confidence; does what boss wants	System thinking and confidence in group
Learning from Peers/Experts	Gets answer from expert, little confidence in peers	Share expertise, use evidence
View of Self as Person	Begrudging loyalty, asks who really cares?	Company's best asset with willingness to give
Success, Challenge, and Failure	No sense of success or challenge; failure brings blame	Complex solutions, considering many angles, risk taking
Change/ Uncertainty	Hard wired, everything keeps recycling, things can be counted exactly	Continually accommodate, change is constant; much is unknown or unknowable
Need for Security	Want contracts to ensure security	Eliminating fear releases a quickness and flexibility, ensuring security

individual needs the capability for systems thinking and for seeing things as moving processes—and to continue learning throughout life. Also, individuals must believe in their own capacities and have the self-confidence to use these capacities in a group.

Learning from Peers/Experts

In common practice, the expert gives the answer. There is little credence attached to peers' suggestions. In a TQM organization, every-one has ownership of emerging solutions; expertise is shared, and learning is collaborative. People base their solutions on evidence or data, rather than on authority. Much of the synergy in organizations comes from the collective release of human capacities.

View of Self as Person

It is customary at the workplace for individuals to see themselves in adversarial relationships with the company. We are driven by a desire to get as much as possible from the company, and we do little without some external pressure. The TQM organization views the individual as one of the company's treasured assets, and people are willing to give of their treasure.

Success, Challenge, and Failure

In organizations today, individuals customarily keep tasks simple; people do not relish challenge. They use failure as an opportunity to blame others. In the transformed organization, success is credited to the hard work of teams of people using quality tools such as flow chart, Pareto chart, force field analysis, control charts, affinity diagram, prioritization matrices, and activity network diagram for dealing with challenge and complexity. People solve problems using information, connections, and analysis. They value risk taking and view failure as an opportunity for growth.

Change and Uncertainty

Currently, people in many organizations have contradictory attitudes regarding change and certainty. Individuals tend to be rigid or hard wired in their thinking and in denial. People resist change. "What goes around, comes around" is a common adage. This attitude leads to a pendulum theory regarding change: Don't take any change too seriously; it's just a passing fad that will cycle back. Also, certainty prevails: everything can be counted and measured.

In the transformed organization, teamwork calls for an openness to change. Individuals need to restructure or accommodate their thinking and be aware of their blind sides and biases. Openness to change is easier when people see change as the constant. In this view, events are movements of the process and everything is in process. The need for certainty is reduced when one believes, with Deming, that the most important things are unknown or unknowable.

Security

In common practice, employees seek security through ironclad contracts, which generally fail to produce that elusive quality. Fear disappears in TQM organizations. Security is a given. Security leads to flexibility. Sustained success is the goal, not guaranteed security.

These comparisons between today's common practices (the predominant management paradigm) and Deming's TQM approach give us a sense of the vast organizational and human resource development changes that companies have to make as they undertake the quality journey.

These comparisons also point out the leadership challenges that exist. They give us an awareness of the personal development issues that teachers face. And they give us, as leaders in education and other business and government organizations, a common ground to understand each other. We have a common language for such TQM topics as continuous improvement, developing teams, and rethinking incentives.

A tremendous amount of work is involved in making the quality transformation in any organization. As companies talk about long-term deployment plans, so schools also need to take seriously Deming's recommendation for a five- to ten-year transformation time frame. It also would be counterproductive and wasteful to apply TQM to current school practices because this would only foster the current practice of predominantly low level learning. By all indications, Goodlad's (1983) description of U.S. schools still holds: they are dominated by English/language arts and math with consistent attention to basic facts and skills. As a result, as the Minnesota Business Partnership Education Quality Task Force (1992) found, "64 percent of Minnesota employers said that although today's applicants were as well educated as applicants of 10 years ago, that was no longer good enough for today's business standards. They no longer met the world-class standards of our international business competitors."

TQM can be applied in any organization doing any type of task and still not produce the results needed. Auto service centers could spend five years continuously improving carburetor repair, which is useless in an era of fuel-injected engines. Hospitals could get better at blood-letting. Just as auto service centers and hospitals must alter their core technologies to adapt to changing conditions, so must schools.

As we begin to consider the new core technologies needed, I find it useful to stay with the task and individual themes. This approach allows us to appreciate the similarities between the foundational thinking underlying the transformed workplace and the type of cognitive behavior underlying most of today's learning expectations for K–12 students. In the next sections, I use the *task* and *individual* themes to compare customary and transformed school settings.

Task Issues of Quality Education

The nature of the problem, motivation, solutions, and other factors associated with tasks are the same for schools' curriculum and instruction as they are for other organizations. Figure 1.5 shows a comparison between customary and transformed views of tasks in school.

The Nature of the Problem

Customary schools continue to emphasize simple cause and effect examples, which hold little explanatory power in this more complex age. For example, basal readers still have lessons in simple cause and effect activities. Forrester (1991) says, "Education does little to prepare students for succeeding when simple, understandable lessons so often point in exactly the wrong direction in the complex real world." New learning expectations call for students to see connections and links that are far distant in both time and space. Students in transformed schools engage in systems thinking (Senge 1990).

FIGURE 1.5
Tasks in School

The Task	Customary Outcomes	Transformed Outcomes
Nature of the Problem	Simple cause and effect	Use systems thinking
Motivation for Task	Perform for grades and recognition	Intrinsically motivated, curious, have joy in learning
Time Frames	Rush for content coverage while working with small, unrelated pieces	Slow nature of conceptual change, long-term woven themes
Nature of Solutions	Simple answers	Ambiguity and complexity valued
Human Capacities Used	Memory the most used capacity; no groups to construct learning	Social construction of knowledge, with criteria validating ideas
Assessing Results	Learn for test, and then forget	Learning generates new learning, as a recursive cycle

Motivation for the Task

Currently, most motivation in school is based on performance and the contingencies surrounding performance, such as grades, teacher approval, and privileges. The transformed school needs to maintain what Deming believes is each individual's birthright. Deming (1992) states, "One is born with intrinsic motivation, self-esteem, dignity, a sense of cooperation, curiosity, and joy in learning. These attributes are high in the beginning of life, but are gradually crushed by the forces of destruction." Deming suggests that the forces of destruction start with grades and gold stars in school. Deming's observations are corroborated by the extensive research on motivation of Deci and Ryan (1985) and Dweck (1986).

Time Frames

In common school practice, time frames revolve around numbers of chapters or units to be completed by the end of the year. Dividing the number of weeks in the school year by the number of chapters generally sets a grueling pace because of a "systems"-imposed, content-coverage mania.

The transformed school site is informed by research that is revealing the importance of constancy of purpose in student learning. Kathy Roth and coworkers (1992) chronicle the slow nature of conceptual change in important areas. These researchers describe disadvantaged students coming to appreciate what science means and what personal power is afforded by thinking like a scientist. Teachers need to have overall guiding themes that are carefully orchestrated and supportive of a subtle student growth throughout the school year (Wineburg and Wilson 1988). This intellectual change must be consistently supported and nurtured over years. Classrooms can't be isolated; faculties must collectively work to foster student development that spans more than one school year or other arbitrary chunks of time.

The Nature of Solutions

Schools currently give students little opportunity to learn problem-solving techniques. The type of problem solving that schools do encourage generally comes from the obvious application of a principle recently taught to a particular situation. This is a type of "near transfer" (Perkins 1992) or application that is much simpler than the solution sets needed for today's problems. In the transformed school, solutions to problems need to consider the complexity and ambiguity of life today—or, for that matter, to consider ambiguity in our past. For instance, who fired the first shot in the American Revolution? A thoughtful solution can only convey uncertainty because historical evidence leaves the matter in doubt. More important, students develop a sense that solutions are not always pat answers.

Human Capacities Used

The predominant human capacity used in today's schools is still *remembering*. Even cooperative groups, when used, generally involve students' coaching each other in remembering. In the transformed school, learning is not just remembering, but is seen from a social construction point of view. Students make meaning from group stimulation and interaction in a free flow of meaning. Students need to be open to new ideas and also facile in employing criteria and conventions that validate ideas and reasoning. David Perkins (1992) fully discusses the idea of *distributed intelligence**: "The work of the world gets done in groups! People think and remember socially, through interaction with other people, sharing information and perspectives and developing ideas" (p. 134).

Assessing Results

Currently, the results of most learning tasks are grades students receive when they take textbook tests or meet narrow behavioral objectives. Procedures are standardized, and we are comfortable with the lack of ambiguity. In the transformed school, the outcomes of learning need

---

*According to Perkins, the term *distributed intelligence* came from a discussion among David Perkins, Roy Pea, Gavrel Salomon, and others at the 1990 meeting of the American Educational Research Association in Boston.

to be understanding, relating, and applying knowledge in problem solving. Perkins (1992) asserts that without an understanding of a topic, students find that the active use of knowledge of the topic comes hard. The rub here is that we have seldom contemplated that our understanding of understanding is incomplete. Our current struggles with authentic assessments are causing us to address this challenge. In addition, learning should generate new learning in a recursive cycle, similar to the PDSA cycle. This could be a true assessment of "learning how to learn."

Individual Issues of Quality Education

Just as customary business management has outmoded ways of viewing the individual, so do our schools today. Do students view themselves as learners? Are they encouraged to learn from their peers, and do they know how to work effectively in groups? How do they obtain self-validation and a feeling of security? In the following sections, I compare the customary and transformed school setting from the perspective of demands on the individual student. Figure 1.6 summarizes these views.

FIGURE 1.6
The Individual in the School

The Individual	Customary Outcomes	Transformed Outcomes
Self as Learner	Accumulate information; find out what teacher wants	See patterns, step beyond paradigms, use strategies, and see recursively
Learning from Peers/Experts	Ignorance in groups; experts should tell	Social construction (meaning from dialogue); experts still growing, too
View of Self as Person	Based on performance	Inherent worth, creative and curious
Success, Challenge, and Failure	Ability and luck, not effort cause success; anxious and defensive; tacit agreements about work demands	Understand that effort causes success, relish challenge, and see failure as learning
Change/ Uncertainty	Little change; veneers of information in inert memory banks; "right" answers	Conceptual change is open to accommodation; complex decisions uncertain with many perspectives
Need for Security	Security in knowing how to pass tests	Security resides in sense of inherent worth; free to craft flexible solutions

17

Self as Learner

In schools today, many students see the learning act as accumulating as much information as possible. The students try to figure out what the teacher wants. A good memory is crucial. Other students, according to Roth (cited in Anderson 1987), try to make sense of their readings but expect the text to confirm their prior knowledge. They read texts to basically verify and add details to what they already know.

In the transformed school site, the learners will need the practice of learning to reconcile the text and other information sources with their prior knowledge. This cognitive conflict will often be resolved by the students' changing their misconceptions in favor of more powerful, sensible disciplinary explanations (Anderson and Roth 1989). This will call for students to be aware of personal strategies for learning, to develop the ability to step beyond the paradigms that limit and bias learning, and to keep beliefs and actions congruous. This has been the challenge of learning for centuries.

Learning from Peers/Experts

In customary practice in U.S. schools, we often question the merit of learning from peers. We believe this is the ignorant teaching the ignorant. Things would be fine if the expert teachers, who know it, would just share their knowledge and tell us what we are to know.

In the transformed school, an important mode of learning is the social construction of meaning. Perkins (1992) described "distributed intelligence" earlier. Meaning is made by challenge and dialogue with peers. Ways of knowing are being considered from many perspectives (Belenkey, Clinchy, and Goldberger 1986; Minnich 1990). Technology is being applied to the social construction of meaning. Computer Supported Intentional Learning Environments (CSILEs) provide a means for a group of students to collect their thoughts into a data base, which is then available to all students in the form of pictures and written notes (Scardamalia, Bereiter, McLean, Swallow, and Woodruff 1989) (see also Chapter 5, in "Connecting Ways of Knowing"). Apple Computers is also working in partnership with other companies to develop personal digital-assistance devices (Newton Technology) that allow thought sharing within groups. These devices, essentially laptop computers working like writing slates rather than typewriters, will allow learning groups to share individual written thoughts and diagrams via an instantaneous, wireless, transmission capability. In this new view of learning, experts are seen as individuals with deeper understanding and residing uncertainties, yet maintaining a proactive stance in their professional lives and a commitment to relativism (Perry 1981). These qualities become apparent to students if they are modeled by the "experts."

Self as Person

Currently, schools focus on performance (Dweck 1986) and thus develop a sense of self-concept in students that is performance centered. Students feel worthy only if they receive good grades. Ironically, most schools' lists of outcomes indicate that developing high self-concepts is a major goal. The transformed school removes what Deming calls the "forces of destruction"—grades, performance appraisals, and excessive evaluations.

Instead, the transformed school focuses discussion on our birthright as individuals—intrinsic motivation, self-esteem, dignity, a sense of cooperation, curiosity, and joy in learning. Such a focus fosters much more of students' inherent potential from the beginning; and young students thus don't need to change their habits as much as adults do. For example, Covey (1989), in *The Seven Habits of Highly Effective People*, advocates an "inside-out" approach to changing paradigms, motives, and character—that is, changing one's own habits first, before trying to change others.' This approach is particularly applicable for adults (especially educators) who have already been affected by the forces of destruction.

Success, Challenge, and Failure

The customary approach to success in our schools includes providing undemanding intellectual tasks that lead students to attribute their success to luck and ability. When students need to exert much effort, they conclude they have little ability. If tasks are challenging, they cause anxiety (Dweck 1986). Often, there are tacit contracts between students and teachers to keep work simple (Doyle 1983). If tasks involve risks of failure, students act up or are defensive and withdrawn.

In transformed schools, it will be more productive for students to attribute their success to effort (Dweck 1986), especially when pursuing tasks for the challenge and understanding they themselves want. When failure occurs, it is valued. It is part of a feedback system, like PDSA, which provides insights regarding where to increase effort and where to rethink strategies.

Change and Uncertainty

In customary practice today, most schooling fails to engage students in conceptual change (Roth, cited in Anderson 1987); rather, schools add layers of new information to inert memory banks. Schools condition students for certainty by reinforcing a "one right answer" mentality.

In the transformed school, learning involves a clear awareness of conflicting information. The new learning expectations call for a restructuring and accommodation of new learning with prior learning. Roth (cited in Anderson 1987) offers clear examples of reading strategies that promote conceptual change and enable students to develop a deep understanding of such concepts as photosynthesis. In the transformed school, students profit from appreciating the tentativeness of many subject areas and an understanding that there are often many perspectives on issues (Paul, Binker, Jensen, and Kreklau 1987). Most complex decisions are made under conditions of uncertainty.

Security

In the current school, a student's sense of academic security depends on knowing the answers to tests in advance. In the transformed school, security resides in the student's sense of personal inherent worth. This type of security, along with a belief in oneself as a learner, allows students to flexibly craft solutions to challenging problems (Dweck 1986).

A Synthesis of Workplace and School Outcomes

A deeper look at Deming's system of knowledge, which goes beyond his fourteen points, allows us to synthesize the task and individual issues for both the workplace and the school. Comparing "customary" with "transformed" practices shows the interrelated changes that are required. Such massive change has deep psychological roots. It is difficult for rigid, hard-wired folks to get excited and, more important, act congruently with the reality that *change is the constant*. Also, it is hard for us, when we've been conditioned to believe in experts' answers, to trust ourselves and our coworkers as problem solvers. Schools will have as much difficulty with this change as any organization. In fact, schools most likely will have more difficulty with the change process—when we consider that little fundamental change has occurred in U.S. education in almost a century. A TQM transformation requires change at a personal level and in the manner in which we approach tasks in our schools.

Any business organization making the quality transformation faces an incredible task (see Figures 1.3 and 1.4). As educators, we face a doubly difficult challenge (see Figures 1.5 and 1.6). While we, too, have to change the work setting, we also must change our core technology—*the teaching/learning process*. Improving the quality of education calls for perfecting new core technologies. More custom crafting of each product (the student) is needed. This development is equivalent to business' making all the personal and organizational changes, plus developing a completely new manufacturing process that depends much less on mass production and more on finding and capitalizing on small, changing "market niches" (Reich 1991b; Toffler 1990). Current education research supports such new core technologies, or educational practices, as active learning, systems thinking, constructivism, intrinsic motivation, and self-concept based on inherent worth.

Much of the old educational paradigm is a contributor to the status quo in business organizations. This claim is supported by considering how the "customary" outcomes of schools fit perfectly with the "customary" practices of the workplace. Figure 1.7 shows this fit for *task* issues by placing these outcomes together; the same can be done for the individual issues.

FIGURE 1.7

Customary Tasks in the Workplace and in School

The Task	Customary Workplace Practices	Customary School Outcomes
Nature of the Problem	Blame people, regulations, and the situation	Simple cause and effect
Motivation for Task	Perform for pay. incentives	Perform for grades and recognition
Time Frames	Quarterly reporting	Rush for content coverage while working with small, unrelated pieces
Nature of Solutions	Please the boss; keep answers simple	Simple answers
Human Capacities Used	Control, one-upmanship, discussion	Memory the most used capacity; no groups to construct learning
Assessing Results	Plan and do with little reflection	Learn for test, then forget

As a point of historical interest, when we examine these outcomes and practices, we can see why schools did such a good job in supplying the skills needed in the old type of organization.

Next, for purposes of comparison, let's examine the same task issues, this time comparing "customary" school practices with "transformed" business practices needed for the future—and, increasingly, for today's workplaces (see Figure 1.8).

It is immediately obvious that the common school practice of today is point by point at odds with what is needed for employee skills and predispositions in the transformed workplace.

Placing the "transformed" practices of schools and workplaces next to each other shows how transformed school outcomes support new business practices that are becoming increasingly common. Figure 1.9 illustrates the correlation between "transformed" outcomes and practices, this time for *individual* issues. The same comparison can be made

FIGURE 1.8

Transformed Workplace Practices
Versus Customary School Outcomes

The Task	Transformed Workplace Practices	Customary School Outcomes
Nature of the Problem	90% is in the system	Simple cause and effect
Motivation for Task	People want to do good job; pride in work	Perform for grades and recognition
Time Frames	Constancy of purpose; 5-10 years to transform	Rush for content coverage while working with small, unrelated pieces
Nature of Solutions	Seeking root causes, complexity, and understanding	Simple answers
Human Capacities Used	Teams responsible; flow of dialogue with assumptions suspended	Memory the most used capacity; no groups to construct learning
Assessing Results	Plan, Do, Study, Act as a continuous cycle	Learn for test, then forget

FIGURE 1.9

Transformed Workplace Practices and School Outcomes

The Individual	Transformed Workplace Practices	Transformed School Outcomes
Self as Learner	System thinking and confidence in group	See patterns, step beyond paradigms, use strategies, and see recursively
Learning from Peers/Experts	Share expertise, use evidence	Social construction (meaning from dialogue); experts still growing, too
View of Self as Person	Company's best asset with willingness to give	Inherent worth, creative and curious
Success, Challenge, and Failure	Complex solutions, considering many angles, risk taking	Understand that effort causes success, relish challenges, and see failure as learning
Change/ Uncertainty	Continually accommodate, change is constant; much is unknown or unknowable	Conceptual change is open to accommodation; complex decisions uncertain with many perspectives
Need for Security	Eliminating fear releases a quickness and flexibility, ensuring security	Security resides in sense of inherent worth; free to craft flexible solutions

for task issues. It is apparent that a multifaceted paradigm shift in schools will be necessary to foster the individual student outcomes of significance that in the future will support the staffing needs of TQM organizations. Transformed school outcomes are foundational for individuals in TQM organizations. We have much work to do to make these practices and outcomes realities in schools.

School conditions and outcomes must change now to support the quality transformation occurring in companies today. Schools are of little help in the quality transformation by only teaching information about quality tools and practices to students. The underlying psychological beliefs and cognitive skills are the true foundations for the quality transformation. Unless this deeper change occurs, schooling will become increasingly irrelevant, if not counterproductive.

We must try to understand the root causes underlying our schools' customary practices and the usual student outcomes. This understanding is essential if we wish to meet education's double TQM challenge. We can't apply TQM to schools as organizations while ignoring the existing teaching and learning practices. Unless we meet the double challenge, we will only be improving the carburetor shop.

Finally, Figure 1.10 combines information from previous figures to show both task and individual perspectives of workplaces and schools and—in a global way—shows the comprehensive changes needed in our schools today. This figure can be useful to education leaders in the following ways as we pursue a quality journey in our school districts:

1. As an education leader, you can converse with business leaders about the changes they are making on their quality journeys.

2. As an education leader, you can develop a mutual understanding with business leaders regarding similar change activities. You can explain the need to radically change the nature of the learning process. If they are impatient, it is important to point out that if schools merely apply TQM to current educational processes—which generally produce low-level learning and do not change the total curriculum and delivery system—their application of TQM will not benefit the business community in the long run.

3. TQM is a process that both business and education must present to the community. The figures in this chapter, particularly Figure 1.10, which synthesizes this chapter's findings, can help you explain the range of changes needed. This could be a way of getting important community understanding of the need for a change in school practices and traditions that most of us have commonly experienced.

4. The figures in this chapter can be used as tools to show educators the kinds of changes companies are making. These changes are often quite different from educators' beliefs about the business world.

5. Using Figure 1.10, teachers can brainstorm what characteristics of the transformed workplace setting could be applied in school. The figures can also help them select some productive places to start the

FIGURE 1.10

Comprehensive Comparison of Customary and Transformed Settings

	WORK SETTING		SCHOOL SETTING	
The Task	**Customary**	**Transformed**	**Customary**	**Transformed**
Nature of the Problem	Blame people, regulations, and the situation	90% is in the system	Simple cause and effect	Use systems thinking
Motivation for Task	Perform for pay, incentives	People want to do good job; pride in work	Perform for grades and recognition	Intrinsically motivated, curious, have joy in learning
Time Frames	Quarterly reporting	Constancy of purpose, 5-10 years to transform	Rush for content coverage while working with small, unrelated pieces	Slow nature of conceptual change, long-term woven themes
Nature of Solutions	Please the boss; keep answers simple	Seeking root causes, complexity, and understanding	Simple answers	Ambiguity and complexity valued
Human Capacities Used	Control, one-upmanship, discussion	Teams responsible, flow of dialogue with assumptions suspended	Memory the most used capacity; no groups to construct learning	Social construction of knowledge, with criteria validating ideas
Assessing Results	Plan and do with little reflection	Plan, Do, Study, Act (PDSA) as a continuous cycle	Learn for test, and then forget	Learning generates new learning, as a recursive cycle
The Individual				
Self as Learner	Challenge seeing process, lacks confidence; does what boss wants	System thinking and confidence in group	Accumulate information; find out what teacher wants	See patterns, step beyond paradigms, use strategies, and see recursively
Learning from Peers/Experts	Gets answer from expert, little confidence in peers	Share expertise, use evidence	Ignorance in groups; experts should tell	Social construction (meaning from dialogue); experts still growing, too
View of Self as Person	Begrudging loyalty, asks who really cares?	Company's best asset with willingness to give	Based on performance	Inherent worth, creative and curious
Success, Challenge, and Failure	No sense of success or challenge; failure brings blame	Complex solutions, considering many angles, risk taking	Ability and luck, not effort cause success; anxious and defensive; tacit agreements about work demands	Understand that effort causes success, relish challenge, and see failure as learning
Change/ Uncertainty	Hard wired, everything keeps recycling, things can be counted exactly	Continually accommodate, change is constant; much is unknown or unknowable	Little change; veneers of information in inert memory banks; "right" answers	Conceptual change is open to accommodation; complex decisions uncertain with many perspectives
Need for Security	Want contracts to ensure security	Eliminating fear releases a quickness and flexibility, ensuring security	Security in knowing how to pass tests	Security resides in sense of inherent worth; free to craft flexible solutions

process, as well as consider the human resource development needed. Further, the "transformed" workplace practices provide a comprehensive overview of the outcomes that students will need in the transformed work setting.

Education and business share the same problems when they embark on the quality journey in pursuit of transformation. It is also apparent that current school outcomes and conditions must be altered if they are to support the transformation occurring in companies and other public organizations.

2

Why Use a Business Approach to Transform Education?

If we had time to listen to a thoughtful group of teachers, involve them in a workshop or exercise on paradigm shifts (such as watching Joel Barker's 1990 video), and ask some probing questions, the teachers might begin to discover, on their own, the foundations of Deming's Total Quality Management (TQM). Imagine the following dialogue with a teacher.

Question: What are some problems you see with inservice?

Response: It's here today and gone tomorrow. It's some theory that doesn't get used in our classrooms.

Question: What might make this better?

Response: We need to stick with things we start (constancy of purpose), and it's good to have chances to practice the new learning.

Question: Why don't we have better coordination between departments and grade levels?

Response: There's just no time! There are barriers and a lack of communication.

Question: What might make this better? Isn't the answer pretty obvious?

Response: Yes, we need more time to talk if we are going to break down the barriers. The few meetings we've had have been tremendously informative.

With this type of teacher dialogue, we could easily get support for all of Deming's fourteen points. But many red flags are raised when teachers hear business leaders suggest that schools use TQM.

Educators are usually skeptical about accepting business panaceas for schools. We often have an integrated set of beliefs and attitudes that cause us to mistrust business. Many of us regard suggestions from businesspeople as meddling. Educators ask: Are we being compromised by business? Isn't there more to an education than what business wants? Haven't the manufacturing accoutrements of measurement, standardization, and mass production already caused problems in education? Look at business; the economy is in bad shape. Are these same business leaders, with dubious success records, trying to tell us, again, how to run our schools? Why should we jump on the TQM bandwagon?

TQM Can Add Dignity and Rigor to the Teaching Profession.

A quality education is at the core of individual and national prosperity. Harvard economist Robert Reich (1991a) describes a rapidly developing world economy where the highest wages (greatest reward) go to specialized knowledge brought to bear on problems, and where solutions define new horizons of possibilities. Reich offers an example:

> A London department store buyer of high fashion apparel orders a line of dresses devised by a New York fashion designer. Within an hour of the order, the designer sends via satellite the drawings and specifications for making the dresses to a fiber optic link in Hong Kong, where they appear on a high-resolution computer monitor, ready for a manufacturing engineer to transform them into prototype garments. The prototypes are then reproduced in a Chinese factory. The designer, the engineer, and the factory supervisor conduct a video conference to work out details, and the finished garments arrive in London less than six weeks after the order is placed. Here, America "exported" a fashion design, and some management services linked the design with the London buyer and the Hong Kong and Chinese technicians (p. 40).

A nation can increasingly export the benefit of skills involved in solving, identifying, and brokering new problems and solutions. This capacity affects the balance of trade. If education can deliver these skills, it will certainly become the centerpiece of our economy. The student coming from the transformed school environment will have the core capacities for success in organizations embracing the TQM movement.

The tired old cliche still persists, "If you can, you do; if you can't, you teach." But the reality is "Those who can, do; those who understand, teach," according to the Stanford Teacher Assessment Project.* Teachers

---

*The Teacher Assessment Project was a research and development initiative in the School of Education at Stanford University designed to generate a set of prototypes for alternative ways to assess teaching. For an overview of this work, see Shulman (1987).

who are successful in school environments will prepare citizens for the new world economy. The key to education is understanding—and understanding is also at the core of Deming. Deming wants people to be very clear on their assumptions or theories, which are at the core of understanding. Deming (1992) says, "Without theory, experience has no meaning. Without theory, one has no questions to ask. Hence without theory, there is no learning." Understanding will be a keystone of success. The teaching profession needs to be based on facilitating learning for understanding.

The previous chapter consists of a wide-ranging discussion of Deming and TQM in terms of paradigm shifts and conceptual change. This "stuff of the mind" is our stock in trade as educators. We need a deep understanding of the psychology and theory of knowledge that underlies Deming's thinking. It is the same foundation that can guide us in changing the school setting and nature of learning. The Deming paradigm does double duty for us. It guides the transformation of the workplace for the teaching profession, as it does for all other professions. But it also can guide the transformation of education into a constructivist, meaning-making, learning environment.

This realization of the double benefits of TQM in education is something we can share as we work with other community leaders who may be trying to implement TQM in their factories, human services systems, retail stores, and other businesses. These leaders know the extensive effort that is called for in TQM implementation. They usually have only a single challenge—to change the nature of their organization's workings. Our second challenge—to improve teaching and learning— can give community leaders an appreciation of an aspect of education that few have considered. Such community awareness can promote in-depth, public understanding of our issues.

TQM recognizes the complexity of systems working together for a quality product or service. We can't keep it simple; it isn't simple. We put more thought into preventing rust in a car door than we do in solving education's complex problems.

TQM can dignify education by allowing us to diffuse the charge that education is at the root of our economic woes. Education need not be the scapegoat for America's economic downturns. However, if education systems fail to embrace TQM, education will be more culpable when companies make the switch and still see an emerging work force being trained in the old paradigm. What do businesses want of our schools?

Business Seeks Graduates with a Sound, Well-Rounded Education.

Often teachers are concerned that educating students to meet business requirements deprives the students of a good education. David Kearns (1988), former chief executive officer at Xerox, addressed this concern:

Lest you think I'm interested in vocational education, let me assure you that nothing could be further from the truth. We need employees who are broadly and deeply educated; men and women who are liberally educated (p. 32).

This is a tremendous challenge. A "deep education" is at the core of our ability as educators to support a productive economy and promote rich civic and personal lives.

There Will Be a Very Strong Push by Society for TQM.

We can try to resist TQM, but we aren't likely to succeed. The quality movement is everywhere. We are constantly hearing about it in advertising. (At Ford, "Quality Is Job One"; at Motorola, "Quality Is Built In Before the Name Goes On"; and Cadillac won the prestigious Malcolm Baldrige National Quality Award.) Now the predictable push is coming. Most business leaders will reason that if the quality movement is making our companies better, certainly it can make schools better, too.

Unions Are Beginning to Buy into the Quality Movement.

In November 1991, the United Auto Workers' official monthly publication, *Making Quality Our Right*, included such comments as:

> We also know that, in the final analysis, our jobs depend on producing quality goods and delivering quality services . . . . (p. 7) Workers are being brought into a new communications network with other workers and their customers, and there is a redefined notion of who a customer is. In parts plants, workers are phoning their customers—workers in assembly plants—to make sure their parts are perfect; in assembly plants, workers are talking with dealers and the public (p. 6).

TQM Can Serve as an Umbrella for Many of the Innovations Valued in Education Today.

TQM provides a planning and development structure to nurture and support innovations in education. This has rarely happened in the past. The next chapter shows how to get started on your TQM journey.

3

The Power of the Malcolm Baldrige Criteria and Leadership

At this stage, you should have some realization of the magnitude of change necessary to implement Total Quality Management. You can begin a dialogue about TQM with school staff, business leaders, and members of the community. But how do you get started on this process with its mammoth commitment? How do you get Deming's fourteen points working together?

Much of the quality transformation in U.S. industry is being influenced by the Malcolm Baldrige National Quality Award. This awards program began taking applications in 1988 and gave its first award in 1989. The Baldrige Award was designed to heighten the quality awareness of U.S. companies and to promulgate successful quality strategies to other companies. The success of the program has mushroomed. Although no more than six companies can receive the award annually, the number of requests for the application forms has risen from 12,000 in 1988 to 65,000 in 1989; 180,000 in 1990; and 235,000 in 1991.

Harvard Business School professor David A. Garvin (1991), an expert on the Baldrige Award, says of its impact:

> In just four years, the Malcolm Baldrige National Quality Award has become *the* most important catalyst for transforming American business. More than any other initiative, public or private, it has reshaped managers' thinking and behavior. The Baldrige Award not only codifies the principles of quality management in clear accessible language, it also goes further: it provides companies with a comprehensive framework for assessing their progress toward the new paradigm of management and such commonly acknowledged goals as customer satisfaction and increased employee involvement (p. 80).

The criteria for the Malcolm Baldrige National Quality Award include leadership, customer focus and satisfaction, strategic quality planning, information and analysis, human resource development and management, quality and operational results, and quality assurance of product and service. Figure 3.1 provides an overview of the criteria and their relationships to each other. I have placed leadership in an "umbrella" position because of its critical role; leadership is the most important quality issue in education. The award application itself is a document of about 40 pages and can be obtained from the National Institute of Standards and Technology.* Each of the seven criteria has approximately five subcriteria. The document submitted as an application can be no longer than 50–75 pages, depending on the size of the organization.

The Chain Reaction Effect

The Baldrige Award is producing a chain-reaction effect in U.S. business. Two of the criteria include requirements for applicants to spread the quality "gospel" as a public responsibility and to diligently work with their suppliers to use quality principles.

Two Baldrige winners, IBM and ZYTEC, have initiated such a chain reaction. In the area of Winona, Minnesota, both companies have made enthusiastic public presentations that have been well attended. The IBM quality director likened learning about the award's criteria to a three-credit Harvard master of business administration course. In Winona, several electronic components suppliers for both ZYTEC and IBM are now also aggressively pursuing quality awards. Leaders from these local companies are logically suggesting the use of TQM in education because they see schools as their own critical suppliers.

In a recent conversation with my local quality mentor, Dan Rukavina of EMD, Inc. I learned about his company's Baldrige applications. Rukavina suggested several benefits from the extensive, tedious award-application process. Foremost was the capacity to visit with other companies on the quality journey and to use a common lens for sharing quality processes. EMD representatives have visited three of the eight Baldrige winners to learn about other companies, in a process called *benchmarking*. Garvin (1991) points out:

> Truly excellent companies use benchmarking as a catalyst and enabler of change, a learning process rather than a score card. They scan the world widely for organizations that are skilled at what they do, visit them to gain a better understanding of their processes and ways of working, and use the findings to stretch their imaginations and develop new ways of operating (p. 91).

---

*National Institute of Standards and Technology (NIST), Route 270 and Quince Orchard Rd., Administration Bldg., Room A537, Gaithersburg, MD 20899.

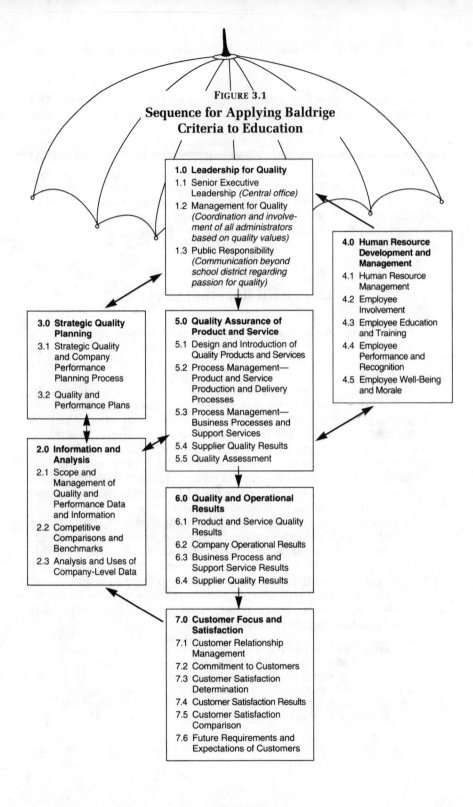

FIGURE 3.1

Sequence for Applying Baldrige Criteria to Education

1.0 Leadership for Quality
1.1 Senior Executive Leadership *(Central office)*
1.2 Management for Quality *(Coordination and involvement of all administrators based on quality values)*
1.3 Public Responsibility *(Communication beyond school district regarding passion for quality)*

4.0 Human Resource Development and Management
4.1 Human Resource Management
4.2 Employee Involvement
4.3 Employee Education and Training
4.4 Employee Performance and Recognition
4.5 Employee Well-Being and Morale

3.0 Strategic Quality Planning
3.1 Strategic Quality and Company Performance Planning Process
3.2 Quality and Performance Plans

5.0 Quality Assurance of Product and Service
5.1 Design and Introduction of Quality Products and Services
5.2 Process Management— Product and Service Production and Delivery Processes
5.3 Process Management— Business Processes and Support Services
5.4 Supplier Quality Results
5.5 Quality Assessment

2.0 Information and Analysis
2.1 Scope and Management of Quality and Performance Data and Information
2.2 Competitive Comparisons and Benchmarks
2.3 Analysis and Uses of Company-Level Data

6.0 Quality and Operational Results
6.1 Product and Service Quality Results
6.2 Company Operational Results
6.3 Business Process and Support Service Results
6.4 Supplier Quality Results

7.0 Customer Focus and Satisfaction
7.1 Customer Relationship Management
7.2 Commitment to Customers
7.3 Customer Satisfaction Determination
7.4 Customer Satisfaction Results
7.5 Customer Satisfaction Comparison
7.6 Future Requirements and Expectations of Customers

Coming from a mindset of industrial espionage and trade secrets, I was surprised to hear about this healthy sharing between companies in corporate America.

In addition to the highly rigorous Baldrige Award, many states are developing state-level award initiatives. The Minnesota Council for Quality has an active state award program, the Minnesota Quality Award (MQA), which is patterned after the Baldrige Award. In Minnesota, 43 percent of all companies with fifty or more employees have established formal quality improvement programs. These businesses are often motivated by the usefulness of the criteria in planning, the learning they do during the process of completing the applications, and the feedback given by the examiners. Minnesota-based Alliant Techsystems uses the award criteria as a mainstay in corporate planning, as follows:

> Initiate Business Process Management as the primary Total Quality Management thrust for Alliant Techsystems.

> Educate employees on the concepts and criteria embodied in the Malcolm Baldrige National Quality Awards guidelines.

> Achieve quality leadership in the defense industry as measured by an internal Malcolm Baldrige score of 600 or greater by July 1993.

The Minnesota Council for Quality has seen very clearly that TQM ideas apply to schools. The Partners for Quality Education Initiative was just completed by the Minnesota Academic Excellence Foundation (MAEF), the Minnesota Council for Quality (MCQ), and the Minnesota Higher Education Board. In a pilot process, including sixteen educational institutions from school districts, community and technical colleges, and state and private universities, participants determined that the Minnesota award instrument and process were appropriate and beneficial for elementary, secondary, and higher education institutions. For K–12 sites, the 1992 Partners for Quality Education Initiative report states: "The process provided a focused framework for reform initiatives, such as outcome-based education (OBE) and site-based decision making" (Buckman and Sharp-Burk 1992, p. 7). The MQA process could open important channels of communication between business and education. An education award category should result in sharing a common language, format, and examiner pool with the existing categories (manufacturing, service, and small business). School districts will be able to apply for the award in the 1993–94 school year. Similar efforts are underway in other states.

Because of the effectiveness and popularity of the Baldrige Award, business leaders are eager to encourage school leaders to engage in a quality award process, which will likely be some offshoot of the Baldrige Award. Realistically, in the no-nonsense business world, many executives will not be excited about the theoretical aspects of Deming's thought. Rather, they will latch on to the nuts-and-bolts criteria of the Baldrige Award. For example, a corporate leader recently told me he knew little about Deming, but everything his company needed to know about quality was included in the Baldrige Award. This attitude is a big mistake, especially for us in education—when there are so many parallels with Deming theory and the changes needed in schools.

In the rest of this book, I describe a process that is a blend of Deming, Baldrige, and contemporary educational research. This process is brief and concrete, yet it is a conceptually sound approach to beginning your quality journey.

Organization of Baldrige Criteria

Beginning in this chapter, I discuss the seven Baldrige criteria as shown in Figure 3.1. The order of presentation and length of description represent my judgment regarding each criterion's relative importance in the educational challenges we face today. Because of its critical importance, leadership is first (see the next section of this chapter). Chapter 4, "Quality Assurance of Product and Service," and Chapter 5, "Human Resource Development and Management," are lengthy and substantive because they make the unique links with the research on teaching and learning—the state of the art for us as educators. Chapter 6 briefly addresses strategic quality planning, information and analysis, quality results, and customer focus and satisfaction. Finally, Chapter 7 describes a deployment plan for schools.

For each of the seven criteria, I highlight three important features:

1. The Deming foundation. Knowledge of Deming's philosophy and fourteen points is essential to the quality journey.

2. Selected examples of considerations under the Baldrige criterion. These examples are representative and brief.

3. The educational implications of the criterion. These implications are essential in guiding the massive change needed in our core technologies (teaching and learning strategies).

The first two features, the Deming foundation and Baldrige criteria, are meant to stand on their own. Familiarity with these two features will allow you to converse with any leader implementing TQM in any type of organization. The third feature, the educational implications, allows you to highlight the specifics regarding the unique core technologies of education. These distinctions are crucial. Well-intended outsiders are attempting to help education by offering their support in improving management practices, through either Deming's fourteen points or the Baldrige criteria. This is well and good—but not enough. If education is to truly serve society's future needs, both education leaders and civic leaders must put much energy into making the necessary changes in our core technologies—teaching and learning. We need to attend to our state of the art. In business parlance, this means having an intimate knowledge of how the manufacturing process out on the shop floor actually works.

Feature 1: The Deming Foundation

The Baldrige Award consistently calls for quality values, but specifies none. This was somewhat of a political response because there are several other quality gurus in the United States, including Joseph Juran, Armand Feigenbaum, and Philip Crosby. I have chosen to stay exclusively with Deming and his value base because of his completeness and deep psychological and philosophical foundation, which parallels many critical educational issues. There is no Deming guide to the Baldrige Award. Deming is strongly opposed to the Baldrige Award principally because of its competitive aspects. In developing the Deming foundation for each criterion, I meticulously catalogued several hundred Deming ideas, principally from his text, *Out of the Crisis* (1986), and then sorted them into Baldrige criteria.

Feature 2: Selected Examples of Points Under the Baldrige Criteria

Immense volumes have been written on tips for completing the Baldrige Award application (e.g., Brown 1992), and consultant work in this area is a growth industry. In coming up with the essence of each criterion, I considered as many as 200 suggestions for the criterion and distilled these down to 6–10 points. This is not a comprehensive list; it is meant only to give representative samples. The educational implications described in Chapters 4 and 5, on the management of process control and human resource development and management, indicate we are probably not ready to quibble over the fine points of completing the application process. Most schools have much work to do in the fundamentals of teaching and learning, education's manufacturing process, before they will do well on awards.

Feature 3: The Educational Implications of Baldrige Criteria

Figure 3.2 shows how TQM can be an umbrella for educational innovation. Segments of the umbrella show the Deming foundation. The umbrella's scallops represent the Baldrige criteria, which provide a means to sort many of the state-of-the-art practices in education today, as shown sheltered under the umbrella. This figure shows that TQM should not be seen as an end in itself, but a means of linking many of today's best educational practices. (See Appendix A for a detailed list of these practices, listed by Baldrige criteria. See also Chapters 4 and 5 for discussions of some of these practices.)

This chapter concludes with a brief consideration of leadership in relation to (1) the Deming foundation, (2) the Baldrige criteria, and (3) the educational implications of the criteria.

I discuss leadership first because this criterion is essential for the quality transformation of American schools. My discussion is brief only

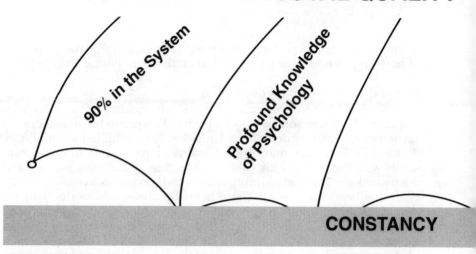

TOTAL QUALITY

90% in the System

Profound Knowledge of Psychology

CONSTANCY

5.0 Quality Assurance of Product and Service

Product

- Effectively use diverse teaching skills, materials, technology, and primary sources
- Manage student groups with a focus on learning
- Use human resources— aides, volunteers, and peer tutors
- Use quality time to plan

Forms of Schooling

- Schools reflect a continuum of flexible structures
- Teachers in grades (K-12) or subjects determine class structures
- Interdisciplinary programming
- Multi-age and interest groupings
- Community-based learning opportunities; school site used only when it's the "best use"
- Students developing learning plans

Process

- Vision includes professionals working together toward continuous improvement of instruction and organization
- Continual upgrading of curriculum and instruction
- Critical appraising of equity and excellence issues
- Fostering school-family collaborations
- Teaming with educational specialists

4.0 Human Resource Development and Management

- Demonstrate (and model for students) lifelong learning, curiosity, careful reasoning, creativity, fairness, respect for diversity, and other character-istics of educated people
- Develop and demonstrate rich, discipline-based, content knowledge
- Develop integrated knowledge, combining skills, dispositions, propositions, and beliefs
- Understand students' perspectives and use effective analogies and illustrations
- Attain skilled use of traditional and performance-based assessments; encourage student self-assessment
- Understand concepts generated by social and cognitive scientists
- Believe that all students can learn

FIGURE 3.2

Educational Implications of Total Quality Management (TQM) and Baldrige Criteria

MANAGEMENT

Ongoing Learning

Continuous Improvement

OF PURPOSE

1.0 Leadership for Quality

Allow teachers meaningful control over conditions of success:

- Provide opportunities for flexible scheduling
- Provide time for growth
- Encourage shared decision making about teaching materials
- Encourage teacher participation in hiring, mentoring, and supporting other teachers

3.0 Strategic Quality Planning

Based on a vision of the *interaction* of all the educational features in Figure 3.2

7.0 Customer Focus and Satisfaction

- Relate to parents constructively
- Convey to students, parents, and the community the belief that all students can learn and the belief in the dignity and worth of all the educational features in Figure 3.2

2.0 Information and Analysis

- With the vision of continuous improvement, find and solve problems; locate, invent, and experiment with different methods of instruction and school organization (see also 5.0, Quality Assurance of Product and Service)
- Track what individual students are learning and *not learning* (not average scores); develop students' abilities in self-assessment (see also 4.0, Human Resource Development and Management)

6.0 Quality and Operational Results

Relate constructively to parents what students are learning, as well as what they are not learning (see also 7.0, Customer Focus and Satisfaction)

Note: See Appendix A for an expanded list of these implications.

because other authors have written extensively about leadership. My intent here is to help educational leaders embrace TQM and apply its principles to the new core technologies of teaching and learning—the heart of this book.

Leadership

Leaders need a deep understanding of the Deming foundation and of the Baldrige criteria.

Deming Foundation

Deming says it is management's job to lead an organization out of crisis. A leader may personally support TQM with a quality values foundation based on the fourteen points. But more important is the consistency between the fourteen points and the day-to-day action of the leader. Top management needs a structure that pushes for TQM daily. Things get better when it is obvious to the employees that management is trying to improve the process. Displaying accomplishments used in assisting employees to improve their performances can be helpful. It may take a minimum of five years to remove impediments and, thus, to allow workers to take pride in their work. This calls for a constancy of purpose.

Deming suggests that leaders must understand that all the alleged external impediments are insignificant compared to those created by people in management themselves. Problems are in the system, so management must know and be responsible for the processes.

Baldrige Criteria

The following Baldrige subcriteria for leadership are particularly illustrative:

• Display quality leadership personally and actively, as recorded in logs or calendars or in employee feedback of leader's involvement in TQM.

• Make TQM the first item on the company agenda.

• Demonstrate an intimate knowledge of how the company actually works.

• Convey a clear, concise mission statement that includes quality.

• Integrate quality values into the organizational approach, as seen in all major decisions.

• Personally train managers in quality and see that they reinforce quality in the workplace.

• Include quality values in all employee training activities.

• Foster cooperation and not competition across functions, maximizing cross-functional teams.

• Communicate quality values to the public.

Educational Implications

The educational implications of the leadership criterion are clear if we seek to transform schools. Education has a unique challenge in applying TQM. Using TQM with existing educational concepts and practices will result in happier students and teachers in a system still driven by low-level learning performance. We will produce a graduate incapable of working in a TQM organization. Currently education is fraught with contradictions, inconsistencies, and discrepancies between espoused values and actual practice. According to Sarason (1990), there is no holistic conception of the system; each group tends to see the problem from a different perspective. We have singular problems in reading, math, science, and self-esteem; few see the big picture. Deming sees this as leadership's challenge; he continually says, "Don't blame the workers. How can they know?"

In many ways, the Baldrige criteria are similar to developmental criteria we are familiar with in education, as described by Piaget, Kohlberg, Gesell, and others. Garvin (1991) describes Baldrige applicants as "beginners" (realize that progress takes time), "bloomers" (showing pronounced spikes but also serious weaknesses), and "more mature adults" (complete integration and consistency, with a distinct personal identity). The TQM organization develops just like the child. Maturity is uneven throughout organizations. It can only be the leader who can get us, as educators, "out of the crisis." We must optimize our system, which is primarily teaching and learning. We need to use what we know from the state of the art in education, rather than complaining about all the impediments.

As I mentioned previously, Chapter 7 provides a deployment plan to show some alternatives in beginning your quality journey. There is much that needs simultaneous attention—and the attention of a leader. One corporate manager told me recently he'd never show the Baldrige criteria to employees—"There's so much there; it would just blow their minds." As educational leaders, we probably have twice as many factors as he does to consider in change. We need to be perfectly clear on our dual needs in changing the school setting (both organizational changes and teaching and learning changes) and be able to explain them to the business community and the community at large. If this common understanding of the challenges is not attained, I believe we might follow some potentially simplistic routes offered to us by well-intended business leaders. Quality awards, especially, require the proper understanding of Deming. He advocates constancy of purpose with long-range time frames. In work as vital and complex as educational transformation, at a minimum, I recommend a decade.

4

Quality Assurance of Product and Service

One of the criteria for the Malcolm Baldrige Award is Quality Assurance of Product and Service. As I stated previously, this criterion strongly relates to *what goes on every day in our schools*, from curriculum to scheduling to teaching strategies—the educational process and the outcomes (products) we expect of our students. How do we assure the quality of our teaching and learning activities? As in Chapter 3 for the "Leadership" criterion, let's look first at the Deming philosophical foundation for this broad area; second, the Baldrige subcriteria; and last, the educational implications.

Deming Foundation

Deming emphasizes an appreciation of the total system. He says that 90 percent of problems reside in faulty systems, not with incompetent people. It is important to set out all the steps necessary to produce quality goods and services. Organizations work best when all workers and managers see the big picture and know how their roles support and are supported by others. The diagram in Figure 4.1 has been Deming's constant reference; he first used it in August 1950 at a conference with Japanese top management on Mount Hakone in Japan.

According to Deming, quality is built in during the design phase; we must not wait to inspect for quality. Quality design comes from knowledge of the process. Solutions do not come from gadgets or slick programs, which are delusionary "instant pudding." Because consumers can't predict their needs three years hence, we must use our knowledge and imagination to anticipate and exceed the customers' wishes.

FIGURE 4.1

The Extended Process

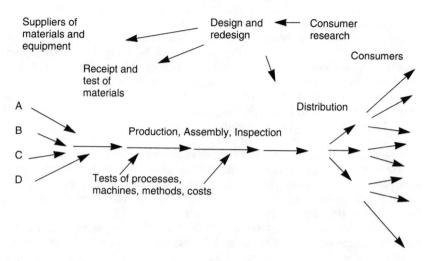

Source: Deming, W.E. (1992). *Leadership for the Transformation in the New Economic Age.* A Four-Day Intensive Seminar, St. Louis, Mo. [Manuscript submitted for publication], p. 37. Reprinted by permission.

Good leadership inquires into causes. It is vital to know the difference between common and special causes and seek process control. It is important to be able to test for several variables.

Continuous improvement is the norm. The suppliers' role is crucial in this improvement. An "arms-around," not "arms-length" approach to suppliers is necessary. The relationship should be established with the supplier long before any material is produced.

Baldrige Criteria

The following guidelines are helpful in assuring the quality of product and service:

• Study the processes involved in production.
• Work with customers to develop standards and design specifications (design in quality).
• Document follow-up of results and systematically correct defects.
• Meet with suppliers to develop improvement strategies.
• Understand who is the customer.

Educational Implications

The criterion relating to quality assurance stresses working with the customers to develop standards and design specifications. Educators engage in two predictable debates: *Who is the customer?* and *What is the nature of the products or services we provide?* The real challenge goes much deeper than negotiating with customers the product or services needed because there is a high degree of surface agreement on that question. The real issue is the lack of in-depth understanding of the processes we need to produce the products or services.

There are several interpretations of who the customer is in education. The national business community sees our international competitiveness slipping and expects a response from education. Is business the customer? Are parents the customers? Is government the customer? It seems to me that the student is the primary customer. We as educators have a role in student development in three overlapping facets of an individual's life: work, civic, and personal.

Considering whether education is a product or service is a moot point, because both are intertwined. Probably more germane is the issue of what I term the *timelessness of a good education.* In Chapter 1, I have cited the National Governors' Association's set of student outcomes. I probably could have just as appropriately cited Cardinal Newman's 1851 description of a well-educated person:

> • [A good education] prepares the person to fill any post with credit, and to master any subject with facility.
> • It gives a person a clear, conscious view of his opinions, and judgments, a truth in developing them, an eloquence in expressing them, and a force in urging them. It teaches the person to see things as they are, to go right to the point, to disentangle a skein of thought, to detect what is sophisticated, and to discard what is irrelevant.
> • The person is at home in any society and has common ground with every class.
> • The person knows when to speak and when to be silent; is able to converse, listen, and can ask a question pertinently and gain a lesson when he/she has nothing to impart . . . and is a pleasant companion and a comrade you can depend upon (Newman 1973, pp. 177–178).

Newman's ideas have striking parallels to futures scanning (Spady and Marshall 1991), which identifies key student graduation competencies: students should be self-directed learners, problem solvers, perceptive thinkers, community contributors, and collaborative workers. The futures-scanning outcomes resemble those of the U.S. Department of Labor Secretary's Commission on Achieving Necessary Skills (SCANS 1991), which calls for competence in resources, interpersonal skills, information, systems, and technology. Alverno College (1990) synthesized a list of graduation outcomes at high school, baccalaureate, graduate, and professional levels, which showed strong similarities (see Appendix B).

Whichever outcomes schools choose to prepare their students for—futures scanning, SCANS, the National Governors' Association, Cardinal Newman, or one of the Alverno options—we can draw parallels between the task and the individual needs in the "transformed" work or school setting (see Chapter 1, Figure 1.10). I suggest not engaging in endless debate about what we want students to know. We could readily come up with 80 percent agreement, but endlessly haggle over the balance. I would hope we can go beyond semantics and get a focus on individual student development by attending to factors that characterize schools on the quality journey. For example, "students in transformed schools are intrinsically motivated, are curious, and show a joy in learning" (see Chapter 1).

As I stated previously, many educators studying Total Quality Management ask questions like "Who is the customer?" and "Is education a product or service?" More important, I believe, is the question "Why has the educational establishment been so unsuccessful in the attainment of the core outcomes most agree upon?" The core is based on higher-level learning, cognitive challenges, and significant problem solving. This latter question switches the discussion to a deeper look at the processes of education.

The observed processes and outcomes of education are succinctly described by Goodlad (1983), who conducted a massive study of classroom practice across the United States. Goodlad found curriculums that were dominated by English/language arts and mathematics, with consistent attention to basic facts and skills from 1st through 9th grades, as well as in the lower track courses beyond 9th grade. The study found that students are not developing the ability to think rationally; the ability to use, evaluate, and accumulate knowledge; or a desire for further learning.

It is ironic that schools across the country look so much alike, even though local control to support our communities' uniqueness and diversity is the backbone of American education. Why do schools look so much alike, and why have they failed in enabling students to attain the outcomes that have been part of the educational rhetoric for years? The answer lies in a deep understanding of educational processes.

Root Causes of Educational Failure

Deming suggests that to lead, one must understand the work. Deming is critical of corporate leaders who just know numbers and do not understand the manufacturing processes. He would likewise be critical of educational leaders who do not understand teaching and learning. Deming suggests that a test of profound knowledge—in any area—is one's ability to continually ask *why* and thus to proceed more deeply into understanding and seeing connections in related areas.

In-depth knowledge about the processes of education suggests root causes. Two educational "root causes" explain much of the failure of educational processes to attain higher level and cognitively challenging learning for students:

1. The pervasive use of textbooks
2. Tacit social contracts between teachers and students

Let's consider the connections between the use of textbooks and current classroom management practices.

Textbooks. Evidence suggests that textbooks cause low levels of learning when they are used as the predominant educational tool. Tyson-Bernstein and Woodward (1989) said that:

> Textbooks have become compendiums of topics, none of which are treated in much depth . . . . [An important] concept is usually "covered" in a drab paragraph or two, which does not allow the author to tell a story that would vivify a principle and fix it in the student's memory (p. 15).

Tyson-Bernstein's insight offers explanation in content areas, such as science, social studies, and health. Failure in basic skills, like learning to read, can also be attributed to poor design in textbooks. Beck (1978) did an extensive review of eight commercially successful and commonly used beginning reading programs. She concluded that whole-word basal readers gave abstract, varied, and inconsistent references and that the lack of concrete pedagogy made it unlikely that low achievers would learn. Shannon (1987) and Goodman, Shannon, Freeman, and Murphy (1988) also fault the prevailing dominance of basal readers. Goodman and coworkers see little value and a host of negative consequences that result from teachers' use of basal readers. Regarding reading failure, they observe, "When children fail to learn to read easily and well through basal instruction, the blame goes either to the teacher for not following the basal carefully or to the children as disabled learners" (p. iv). Perhaps much of the rework that needs to be done in compensatory reading programs could be the result of poor design in beginning reading programs (Schenkat 1988) or the fact that basals are used at all.

Although designing in quality is becoming more prevalent in industry, there is little evidence that quality is designed into textbooks and other commercial material. Even the small amount of prototype testing that is done doesn't have learner verification data to show effectiveness of the materials with different ranges of students under varying conditions (Woodward and Komoski 1987).

This information on the quality of textbooks is important because of the extensive dependence on basal material. Time after time, studies have revealed that, in most subject areas, textbooks define the scope and sequence of curriculum. The textbook structures from 75 to 90 percent of the classroom instruction time (Educational Products Information

Exchange [EPIE] 1976). Lest you think I am overgeneralizing, studies have found little variation in textbooks from different publishers. For example, Stigler (1987) noted a .95 overlap between the objectives of two major math series that represent approximately 40 percent of the market.

Why are textbooks so heavily used? Let's get at some other issues of understanding. U.S. teachers have little time for planning and curriculum design. In contrast, Japanese and Taiwanese teachers spend several hours daily on planning (Stevenson and Stigler 1992). Also, there is truth to the educational adage that "you get what you test for." Often textbooks have supporting assessment systems; both are marketed together. These assessment systems seldom call for high levels of thought; often they consist of multiple-choice items. For instance, a reading comprehension assessment that claims to assess student growth in cause and effect, drawing conclusions, and inference may have little discrimination between the test items from grade to grade or within the comprehension strands. For example, a small action-research study (Schenkat 1987) showed that 2nd graders did almost as well as 6th graders, and students of perceived low ability did almost as well as high achievers on a sequence of mixed comprehension items.

Tacit Social Contracts. Tacit social contracts between teachers and students are also a reason for the low level of cognitive challenge in schools. Doyle (1986) states that students' perceptions of risk and challenge offer additional explanations for the failure of educational processes beyond basic skills learning:

> Tasks involving higher cognitive processes of understanding, reasoning, and problem formulation are high in inherent ambiguity and risk for students. Because the precise nature of correct answers cannot be predicted and rehearsed in advance, the possibility of failure is high. Ambiguity and risk, in turn, shape students' attitudes toward the work they do in classrooms. [Mayers and coworkers] found that high school students' had more positive attitudes and higher motivation in 'boredom' classes in which the challenges were perceived as less than their skills, than in 'worry' classes in which the challenges were perceived as greater than their skills (pp. 406–407).

Doyle also states that when students perceive "ambiguity and risk" in assignments, they "respond by attempting to increase the explicitness of product specifications and reduce the stringency of accountability requirements." Doyle continues:

> Such actions tend to slow down the flow of classroom events, reduce work involved, and increase the frequency of misbehavior and disruption. That is, students' reactions to work create pressures on management systems. In response to disorder in the classroom, teachers often simplify task demands and/or lower the risk of mistakes . . . . In contrast, relatively simple and routine tasks involving memory or algorithms tend to proceed quite smoothly in class with

little hesitation or resistance . . . . In addition, neither teachers nor students talk much about meaning, purposes, or underlying operations of the content, and students seldom receive corrective feedback when they make errors. Although there is often an appearance of engagement, the working is often counterfeit, that is, faked or done without understanding (Doyle 1986, p. 417).

Why would high school students be more motivated and positive in boring classes than in challenging classes? Digging deeper into our knowledge base in this area, Dweck (1986) contends that current educational practice creates high-confidence performers by programming for frequent success and praise. She suggests that a sizable portion of high achievers are performance-goal driven. Because elementary school is not intellectually demanding enough, high school students tend to avoid challenging courses or become anxious and collectively resist the teacher.

Doyle's research bridges classroom learning and classroom management in some provocative ways. McCaslin and Good (1992) point out a paradox concerning the processes underlying a more cognitively challenging curriculum:

> There is consensus that something is amiss in an education that does not include problem solving, integration, and elaboration of meaning . . . . Current beliefs, however, are that a problem-solving orientation should undergird the education of all students, regardless of age, ability, or location . . . . There is a fundamental mismatch in the promotion of a problem-solving curriculum within the context of behavior control management. We cannot expect that students will profit from the incongruous messages we send when we manage for obedience and teach for exploration and risk taking (p. 12).

McCaslin and Good (1992) call for a fundamental shift in classroom management. As we move from basic skills learning (essentially low level) to challenging, problem-solving learning, we can be successful only if students develop internal control and self-regulated learning. Dweck (1986) indicates that students who have developed "learning" goals—even lower-ability students—use failure and obstacles as cues to increase their effort and analyze and vary their learning strategies. Pride in both success and failure is related to the degree of effort they perceive in themselves. On the other hand, students who have "performance" goals are proud of their low-effort mastery but quickly lose confidence when they are challenged. Many of these students dislike taking risks and avoid failure—and thus avoid learning from their experiences.

As we become serious in promoting problem solving and self-regulation, we see the profound wisdom of Jerome Bruner (1962), writing on reward and punishment:

> One of the most important ways to help children think and learn is to free them from the control of rewards and punishment. By

learning what to do to get rewards and by doing just what the teacher wants, children become overachievers, but they will fail to develop the capacity to transform learning into flexible, useful cognitive structures (p. 88).

Implied in Bruner's observation are sophisticated methods of teacher management and an understanding of student development of useful cognitive structures. We are developing a rich understanding of how students come to make meaning. We are beginning to infer the cognitive structures they create. For instance, Kathy Roth (cited in Anderson 1987) reveals dramatic differences in 7th graders' meaning making in a science reading assignment. Almost all students could complete the assigned task and comply with school expectations. Most were confident in their work. Yet, paradoxically, the few students who engaged in true conceptual change were the least confident, feeling confused—while those who only remembered information felt confident. Many practices in our core technology will be changing to encourage self-confidence in students who take risks and make their own meaning.

Developing Cognitive Structures

The process of developing cognitive structures is at the core of the increasingly popular educational concept termed *constructivism*. The success of constructivism, in turn, depends heavily on how well teachers know their content domains in the three areas described by Shulman (1986): content knowledge, pedagogical content knowledge, and curricular knowledge.

Content Knowledge. The first, content knowledge, is the foundation—understanding the content's substance: facts, central organizing principles, and ways new knowledge is created. This seems straightforward but involves more than memorized facts and definitions. "It includes understanding principles and generalizations, trends and sequences, methods for deriving knowledge, theories and structures, and the classification systems and criteria for a given discipline as set forth in Bloom's Taxonomy" (Schenkat and Tyser 1986). Deming's system of profound knowledge is a good example of a person's clarity regarding content knowledge. His profound knowledge is based on an understanding of theories of systems, variation, knowledge, and psychology. Profound knowledge includes understandings of a network of processes or systems, different kinds of uncertainty in statistical data, theories of knowledge, and explanations of motivation.

Shulman (1986) gives an example of what this knowledge might look like for a biology teacher:

> There are a variety of ways of organizing the discipline: (a) a science of molecules from which one aggregates up to the rest of the field, explaining living phenomena in terms of the principles of their

constituent parts; (b) a science of ecological systems from which one disaggregates down to the smaller units, explaining the activities of individual units by virtue of the larger systems of which they are a part; or (c) a science of biological organisms, those most familiar of analytic units, from whose familiar structures, functions, and interactions one weaves a theory of application. The well-prepared biology teacher will recognize these alternative forms of organization.

The same teacher will also understand the rules of biology. When competing claims are offered regarding the same biological phenomenon, how has the controversy been adjudicated? The teacher need not only understand that something is so; the teacher must further understand why it is so, on what grounds its warrant can be asserted, and under what circumstances our belief in its justification can be weakened and even denied. Moreover, we expect the teacher to understand why a given topic is particularly central to a discipline whereas another may be somewhat peripheral (p. 10).

Pedagogical Content Knowledge. The second content domain required of constructivist teachers, pedagogical content knowledge, builds on the content foundation in two ways:

• It is the understanding of what makes specific topics easy or difficult—the conceptions and preconceptions that students of different ages and backgrounds bring to a learning situation. Pedagogical content knowledge requires the use of illustrations, examples, explanations, anologies, metaphors, and demonstrations to make the subject comprehensible.

• It requires the ability to reorganize the understanding of learners or the current meaning learners have made if they have misconceptions.

Pedagogical content knowledge, although the bailiwick of the teacher, also seems to be a useful tool in any individual's communication.

Curricular Knowledge. The third content domain, curricular knowledge, is an awareness of effective programs and teaching materials for particular subjects and topics. It also involves knowledge of what students are studying currently in other courses, what was taught in preceding years, and what will be taught in succeeding years.

Curricular knowledge relates most directly to the school as an organization. All teachers and staff must appreciate the extended process and operate with regard for their "internal customers." For example, in the current school setting arrangement, 3rd grade teachers are the customers of the 2nd grade teachers. Deming stresses how important it is for individuals in all departments to learn about each other and be aware of all the relevant departmental issues. All workers need chances to see the next step in the operation so they know their internal customers.

Producing internally controlled, self-regulated, learning-oriented students (truly self-directed learners) involves an understanding of the extended process. School rules and structures need to be adjusted so that students progressively assume more self-control. This calls for a carefully planned, understood, and monitored process throughout a school building in which teacher behavior, school rules, tasks, and expectations change from lower to upper grade levels. Currently, kindergarten students—through the increasingly common use of learning centers, contracts, and group projects—are often given more opportunities for self-regulated learning than are 3rd grade students. Students in the upper grades should have more, not fewer, opportunities to direct their own learning and to take on challenging tasks. And it is essential that all students in elementary grades experience self-regulated learning if they are to succeed in the complex tasks required in future, "transformed" high schools and the workplace.

* * *

In using state-of-the-art educational strategies, the professional teacher must understand the interactions among motivation, including effort and failure; emerging cognitive structures shaped by subject understanding; and the role of classroom management. Current research is suggesting the interdependence needed among teachers within a school site if this level of student development is to take place. The complexity of this type of cognitive development in students cannot come without a well-integrated effort in the school building. We must adopt new ends and means in education.

The end, or goal, of our educational system has too often been to dole out information in such a way that most students would absorb it well enough to pass the test, to get by, to get through the day with as little disruption as possible. The means to this end involve a pervasive use of textbooks and minimal time to plan. Students and teachers have implicit social contracts; students are motivated in boredom, and they act out in situations involving challengeand ambiguity. The daily work process of the classroom is counterfeit; students want (and get) easy work. Currently, there is little intellectual challenge, especially in the early grades.

In education today, we have new ends in sight: problem solving of original problems and self-directed learning. The means to these ends involve many discipline-based sources: experiences, challenges, and content from varied sources provide the fuel for cognitive structures. Teachers plan together to provide these experiences and sources of information, knowledge, and skills. Motivation for both teachers and students arises from challenging tasks that call for learning from effort and failure.

The Baldrige criteria also suggest meeting with suppliers to develop improvement strategies. In education, parents take the role of supplier in the two parts of learning readiness (Minnesota Business Partnership 1991):

• Students should enter the school system with a rich background developed from home modeling of an interest and curiosity in learning.

• Students should come to school every day ready to learn as a result of proper sleep, nourishment, psychological support, and so forth.

Several important issues arise in dealing with parents as suppliers. For instance, the parent's own educational history might not create a comfort zone in interacting with the school; the parent's own life might be filled with instability; or the parent might not have literacy skills. Although working with "suppliers" deserves a significant amount of attention in optimizing the system, our first obligation is to the quality of our own "manufacturing processes"—the core technologies of teaching and learning.

5

Human Resource Development and Management

Discussions of teachers as human resources are at the heart of the educational process improvement for learners. Both Deming and Baldrige place great emphasis on developing human resources in business; the same is certainly necessary for education. Yet U.S. teachers are part of a "not-quite" profession. Many states still issue emergency certificates long after the emergency has disappeared. Many schools assign the newest, greenest teachers to the most difficult classes—and then offer these teachers very little coaching, mentoring, or incentive to stay. Teacher burnout rates are high—particularly in the first five years of teaching. (For a lucid discussion of the condition of teaching today, see Darling-Hammond and Goodwin 1993.) How can TQM help with human resource development in education? W. Edwards Deming has a great deal to contribute on this topic.

Deming Foundation

Deming contends that the greatest waste in America is the underuse of human talent. In fact, he suggests that a company inventory of knowledge should be listed as an asset on the balance sheet. There should be constant study to optimize the allocation of human effort. Workers need to know the next step in the process, and they are entitled to job satisfaction and self-fulfillment. Deming asserts that absenteeism is a function of less than optimal management.

Deming believes that merit pay, piecework, and number quotas are forces of destruction. Fear must be driven out of the organization so that individuals feel secure. Annual ratings only cause fear. Performance ratings based on a competitive scale have been the ruination of many individuals. Merit pay rewards those doing well in a "stable system," where variation (such as high performance) happens by chance. In keeping with constancy of purpose, Deming asserts that outstanding performance should be rewarded only after long periods—say, seven years; and job hopping should be frowned on. Deming advocates evaluation by listening to the worker for as long as four hours rather than judging by numbers.

A learning community is central to Deming's thinking. The leader needs to understand the company from top to bottom before instituting training. There should be a norm encouraging education and self-improvement; and all individuals should reflect daily on what they learn and sharpen their wits by asking questions. A culture of learning is the foundation for Quality Circles. Teams started without a culture of learning are a sham.

Baldrige Criteria

The Baldrige Award criterion of human resource development and management includes the following subcriteria:

• Plan for increasing empowerment, risk taking, and innovation.

• Involve employees in developing their own performance measures and recognition systems.

• Provide a timely feedback system.

• Value custom-crafted training provided when needed (just-in-time training).

• Emphasize coaching and application in training.

• Determine all levels of employee educational needs and weave these levels into a company plan that includes specific individual plans.

• Honor teamwork as a way of life, with an emphasis on cross-functional work.

• Follow up to see that quality suggestions get implemented or responded to.

• Improve continually in Human Resource Development.

Educational Implications

When Baldrige examiners visit a company, they search for appropriate education and training. Quality training is four faceted:

1. Awareness of the quality movement
2. Use of problem-solving tools (statistics and data analysis)
3. Development of group-process skills (leading meetings, teamwork, making presentations)
4. Development of job-specific skills

As educators, we have much to learn in the first three areas. However, if we wish to accomplish the new product standards (i.e., produce self-directed, lifelong learners), the single most important area is the learning of job-specific skills.

Job-Specific Skills: Ways of Knowing

In attaining new standards for students, we face extensive human resource development implications for ourselves. The phrase "job-specific skills" does not adequately suggest the degree of change we will need to make. It is more than adding another skill to a well-developed repertoire, as you would add a new fairway wood to your golf bag. Rather, the changes necessary are like learning a completely new and very different game. These changes represent new ways of thinking and acting that are contrary to current modes of school delivery. This is an incredible human resource development challenge. The changes we need truly are paradigm shifts.

Extensive research indicates that not only do we not have these job-specific skills—but we don't know we don't have them. Goodlad (1979) found that teachers readily affirm they are developing an array of complex intellectual processes: forming hypotheses, making comparisons, understanding sequence, formulating generalizations and conclusions, and using imagination. Yet Goodlad's classroom observations revealed low levels of thinking and cognitive challenge. In Deming terminology, we do not possess the profound knowledge that undergirds our manufacturing processes. This understanding is necessary to develop teacher "job skills" training to meet the needs of learners today.

Why is there such a discrepancy between what we think we are delivering in schools and what we are actually providing? I suggest three reasons:

1. Few teachers have learned content beyond facts.

2. Levels of adult cognitive development, or conceptual paradigms, affect teacher performance.

3. Many educators hold limited views and beliefs about learning.

These three reasons, which have many similarities, play a part in teachers' ways of knowing, or *epistemology*—which is the study of the origin, nature, methods, and limits of human knowledge.

Kitchner (1986) describes ways of knowing in more detail:

> [Epistemology is] individuals' understanding about what can and cannot be known, how they come to know something (through experience, research, intuition) and how certain they can be of knowledge. These assumptions influence how [people justify] their beliefs, as well as identifying and defining problems, seeking solutions, and revising their problem-solving behavior (p. 76).

Epistemology is not a topic commonly talked about in teacher lounges or presented on inservice days. But it is central to the provision of a challenging, high-level curriculum. Epistemology is related to success in the transformed school site or workplace. More background on the three overlapping ways of knowing—content knowledge, conceptual paradigms, and views and beliefs about learning—provide an appreciation of the challenge we face in human resource development.

Few Teachers Have Learned Content Beyond Facts. This is an incredibly strong indictment. When we look beyond rhetoric to actual practice, the reality of this claim begins to settle in. Arnold Arons, professor emeritus at the University of Washington, has tried, throughout a distinguished career, to understand the challenge of higher-level conceptual learning at the college level and how to transfer such learning to K–12 science teachers.

Arons (1985) explains fact-driven learning:

> We professors proceed through these materials at a pace that precludes effective learning for understanding . . . . Under such pressure, students acquire no experience of what understanding really entails. They cannot test their "knowledge" for plausible consequences or for internal consistency; they have no sense of where accepted ideas or results come from, how they are validated, or why they are to be accepted or believed. In other words, they do not have the opportunity to develop habits of critical thinking . . . and they acquire the misapprehension that knowledge resides in memorized assertions, esoteric technical terminology, and regurgitation of "received" facts. Although such failure is widely prevalent in sciences, it is by no means confined there. It pervades our entire system, including history, the humanities, and the social sciences (p. 143).

Ball and McDiarmid (1990) suggest what this emphasis on remembering facts and lack of understanding could mean for prospective history teachers.

> Student encounters with the disciplines in liberal arts courses likely shape their notions of the nature of the subject matter, as well as their disposition to think about and find out more about ideas in a given field. Imagine the difference between prospective teachers who experience history as an argument about what happened in the past and why, and those who encounter history as what is represented in a textbook? (p. 444).

Ball and McDiarmid (1990) also cite compelling research on the lack of understanding by prospective mathematics teachers. In a sample of 252 preservice elementary and secondary mathematics teachers,

> researchers found that both elementary and secondary majors had difficulty remembering particular ideas and procedures. Moreover, many were unable to make conceptual sense of the mathematics they had learned to perform. In seeking to "explain particular mathemati-

cal concepts, procedures, or even terms, the prospective teachers typically found loose fragments—rules, tricks, and definitions. Most did not find meaningful understanding" (Ball and McDiarmid 1990, p. 442, citing Ball 1990).

Findings like these have astounding implications for teachers. How is it possible for us to teach for understanding when we ourselves do not understand? Ball and McDiarmid (1990) further note:

> Because teachers' work is centrally involved with knowledge and the life of the mind, their own intellectual qualities are extremely important. Teachers must care about knowing and inquiry. They must be able to grapple with fundamental questions about ideas and ways of knowing, and to know the kinds of questions and problems on which different disciplines focus (p. 443).

New paradigms of learning call for teachers to go beyond dependence on commercial materials to create learning experiences for students within and across disciplines. Perhaps this dependence is a function of busy schedules. However, a deeper look suggests that teachers have little background in curriculum development. Typical teacher education programs seldom prepare teachers to be curriculum designers. Heidi Jacobs (1989), an expert in interdisciplinary curriculum development, says, "The starting point for all discussions about the nature of knowledge in our schools should be a thorough understanding of the disciplines" (p. 7). Do U.S. teachers have the job skills to design curriculum in one curriculum—let alone several subject areas simultaneously?

A final indictment of current teacher education programs is that most courses fail to assist prospective teachers in changing strongly held conceptions of learning formed prior to college. It has been commonly accepted that teacher education has little effect (Zeichner and Tabachnik 1981) because of the powerful effect of the school culture once a teacher begins to teach. Ball (1990) posits another explanation in which teacher education or liberal arts coursework never overcomes the powerful effects of K–12 schooling and the wider cultures on prospective teachers. Supporting this claim, Shulman (1991) cites the strong images of teaching and learning held by young children. These images are apparent as preschoolers act out teacher-student situations in play settings.

In contrast to these consistent and common findings, the following descriptions show how teachers could know their content domains in the areas of social studies, English, and mathematics. (See Chapter 4, in "Developing Cognitive Structures," for a discussion of science content.) These descriptions, excerpted from full case descriptions collected from the Stanford Knowledge Growth in Teaching Project, offer standards of excellence or, in TQM terms, benchmarks of performance.* This project

---

*The research reported in these papers was conducted under a grant from the Spencer Foundation to Stanford University for the "Knowledge Growth in Teaching Project," Lee S. Shulman, principal investigator. Descriptions reprinted by permission.

set the research foundation for the standards being evolved by the National Board of Professional Teaching Standards (Shulman 1991).

- *Exemplary Content Knowledge in Social Studies*

Chris was wonderfully articulate about his discipline. He revealed that his interest in anthropology began while he was reading Joseph Conrad. He illustrated the link between literature and human evolution by citing Conrad's Heart of Darkness. Exhibiting an admirable grasp of anthropological perspective, Chris drew and explicated a conceptual map of early human development. Fueling this sophisticated understanding of human evolution was a passionate interest in looking at man and ways of describing man. Anthropology captured Chris' imagination and his interest and his enthusiasm for it is expressed in his teaching.

- *Exemplary Content Knowledge in English*

Always an avid reader, Colleen entered college with the intention of majoring in English. In four years, she completed both her BA and MA in English. Altogether, Colleen took twenty-four English courses; her greatest expertise lies in 20th century American fiction. She brings to her study of English a keen love of words and an awareness of the possibilities of language. Her orientation to English centers around the text itself. In interpreting a story, she refers constantly to the text, reading passages aloud, sometimes several times, to support her points. She prefers literature that is subtle, evocative yet somewhat ambiguous. For this reason, Colleen prefers writers such as Chekhov, Woolf, and Faulkner to such writers as Hemingway or D.H. Lawrence.

- *Exemplary Content Knowledge in Mathematics*

Joe's discussions of mathematics as a field of inquiry revealed an impressive breadth and depth of knowledge of the discipline. He gave long explanations of what math is all about, interweaving historical and structural descriptions. Historically, according to Joe, mathematics began with two basic operations, counting and measuring—that is, numbers and geometry. Each of these led to increasingly differentiated and sophisticated systems. Structurally, he described mathematics as consisting of three branches—analysis, geometry, and algebra—undergirded by logic and foundations. These branches intersect to enrich each other and to form subfields, such as algebraic geometry. For Joe, all these ideas relate to each other . . . . The different parts of mathematics aren't really so isolated.

Joe would be a logical choice to head a math curriculum development team. The chances of developing an interdisciplinary curriculum, relating big themes, would be greatly enhanced if teachers like Joe, Colleen, and Chris could work together. These three teachers go beyond the common bill of fare of college understanding described by Arons (1985). Content knowledge has a direct bearing on a teacher's ability to foster student learning. The contrast between Joe and another teacher in this study, Sharon, makes this abundantly clear.

> Joe consistently explained mathematical procedures very deliberately, step by step, taking little for granted. His language was unfailingly accurate; he used counterexamples to delimit definitions, and also sometimes employed figurative language to explain by analogy . . . . In the instructional segment . . . on factoring quadratic trinomials, for instance, he presented one procedure, gave three examples, then showed a variation of that procedure, followed by three more examples. In two other instances, when some students leaped ahead to the answer to a problem, Joe acknowledged their insight but then went back and supplied the intermediate steps for the rest of the class. Several times Joe responded to students' confusion by reteaching an idea or lesson, acknowledging aloud that the material was not easy. He also diagnosed individual difficulties. By listening carefully, Joe quickly discovered and corrected misconceptions. His extensive knowledge of mathematics was apparent in his teaching in many ways.

* * *

> Sharon, in planning, tried to think about where the students would have problems and tried to come up with at least one extremely clear example that ties main concepts together. She also tried to use examples that represented the types of problems that students would encounter in the homework assignment. But planning for student difficulties and developing clear examples proved more difficult than Sharon expected . . . . Although Sharon recognized the value of being able to provide clear examples, she expressed uncertainty about how to develop that skill; she viewed it as an inherent ability of particular teachers. When students needed help with a problem, she chose to work out the problem for them rather than making the student reason it out. Reflecting on the problems of the group test in her 4th period class, Sharon pointed to the diverse ability level of the students, the language barriers, and the social problems of some students.

Joe and Sharon are markedly different in their capacities with pedagogical content knowledge—understanding what makes specific topics easy or difficult, having a battery of examples and counterexamples, and recognizing whatever student misconceptions are present. Sharon rationalized her difficulties and had little insight into how content knowledge like Joe's could be learned to increase her effectiveness. Moreover, Sharon's explanation of her 4th period results suggests a well-tuned defensive routine that results from her limited sense of personal efficacy.

From these examples, we see that teachers have varying degrees of content knowledge regarding subject matter and its interaction with teaching and learning. The more we expect students to learn for understanding, the more necessary extensive teacher knowledge will be.

Conceptual Paradigms Affect Teacher Performance. Extensive research in adult cognitive paradigms has been done, using the models of Perry (1981); Harvey, Hunt, and Schroder (1961); Basseches (1984); and Belenky and co-workers (1986). Some of this research applies specifically to teaching. Figure 5.1 synthesizes the cognitive models of Perry and Harvey and coworkers, showing the characteristics of individuals at four levels—System 1 through System 4.

The research of Murphy and Brown (1970) contrasts System 1 and System 4 teachers and explains how they differ when conducting the learning process in their classrooms.

- *System 1 Teachers*:

consider themselves, textbooks, and persons in high positions to be sources of authority. Questions have only one right answer. It is inappropriate and unnecessary for students to search for other answers and thereby defy authority. Teachers who function at this level deliver information and ask questions in such a way that only one answer is right. Students are rewarded for recalling the definitions and facts provided by the authoritative sources, and for conforming to the rules and procedures set forth by the teachers.

FIGURE 5.1

Four Cognitive Models, Reflecting Views About Teaching and Learning

System 1

- Black/white vs. shades of gray
- *(Right/wrong answers—knowledge is absolute)*
- Difficulty generating alternatives
- Prefers structured chain of command
- *The teacher is expert*

System 2

- Negative against rules
- Resists control
- Still hard to see another point of view

System 3

- Sees how points of view relate
- A people person, so tasks usually slip
- *All opinions are equally valid*

System 4

- Can accommodate change
- Highly integrated information-processing systems
- Negotiates with others to work out abstract problems
- Good balance of task and personal orientations
- *Sees the big picture in learning (teacher has expertise)*

Note: Items in italic apply particularly to customary teacher outlooks for each system.

Source: Schenkat, R. (1987). "The New Corporate Mind—Empowering Students, Teachers, and Administrators to Develop and Use It." Paper presented at the Annual Conference of the Association for Supervision and Curriculum Development, New Orleans.

• *System 4 Teachers*:

see knowledge as tentative, not absolute, and they have respect for doubt, an openness to new experience, and can consider situations from the pupil's point of view. They do not regard themselves as authority sources. Rules and standards are neither arbitrary nor imposed; rather, they are presented as information. They encourage students to test, relate, and reflect upon their own ideas and to hypothesize, synthesize, and even conjecture about content and ask questions to aid in the search for understanding and for relationships rather than for precise, correct answers (p. 531).

Harvey's (1970) research indicates that few teachers resemble the System 4 description, which is quite similar to goals for high school graduates today (see Figure 5.2).

Also, teacher education graduates do not differ that markedly from liberal arts majors on conceptual positions. Glickman (1986) noted a reduction over the past decade in the percentages of System 1 teachers; these percentages, however, have stayed high, given current expectations for students.

System 1 teachers align with the "customary" school setting described in Chapter 1, whereas System 4 teachers align with the "transformed" school setting. It is not difficult to see which type of teacher would be open to the notion of continuous improvement.

Another set of conceptual descriptors comes from Glickman's (1986) discussion of the three levels of teacher thought: low abstract, moderate abstract, and high abstract (based roughly on the work of Harvey et al. 1961). These descriptors provide an accurate view of a teacher's role in working with a team of peers from a school site or district:

Low Abstract [System 1]:

• Confusion about instructional problems
• Lack of ideas about what can be done
• Often asks to be shown
• Habitual and unilateral responses to varying situations
• Dependent on authority or expert to make change

Moderate Abstract:

• Identification of instructional problems by focusing on one dimension of problems but does not use multiple sources of information
• Generation of one to three ideas about what can be done
• Needs assistance from authority or expert in weighing the consequences of action and planning how to implement change

High Abstract [System 4]:

• Identification of instructional problems from various sources of information

FIGURE 5.2

Conceptual Positions of Liberal Arts
Majors and Teachers

	System 1	System 2	System 3	System 4
Liberal Arts Majors	35%	15%	20%	7%
Preservice Teachers	45%	5%	25%	5%
Inservice Teachers	55%	—	15%	4%

Note: Totals do not equal 100% because of some category overlap. Harvey, Hunt, and Schroder (1961) also found most administrators in System 1, with few in System 4.

    • Seeks and generates multiple sources of ideas about what can be done
    • Visualizes and verbalizes consequences of various actions
    • Chooses for oneself the action(s) most likely to improve the situations and plans implementation
    • Makes own change (Glickman 1986, p. 9).

Teachers face much difficult, personal work in changing from System 1 to System 4 in conceptual thinking. Stephen Covey (1989), in *Seven Habits of Highly Effective People*, states:

> Change—real change—comes from the inside out. It doesn't come from hacking at the leaves of attitude and behavior with quick-fix personality ethic techniques. It comes from striking at the root—the fabric of our thought, the fundamental, essential paradigms, which give definition to our character and create the lens through which we see the world (p. 18).

Many Educators Hold Limited Views and Beliefs About Teaching and Learning. Many teachers seem to have little awareness of a need to learn more than teaching methods. Yet teachers must care about knowing and inquiry in the new paradigm. Most teacher education candidates think they know their content from their high school courses; all they want are some "methods" to teach it. Goodlad (1990) describes the "bag lady" phenomenon, in which teacher education candidates just want more "methods" to put in their bag of tricks. This belief limits school staff development because it perpetuates a mentality that seeks no theory or rationale—just new methods to use Monday morning. Deming sees this kind of learning without theory as pointless.

There is little evidence to support the notion that teachers come to their assignments with the job skills and predispositions to act as members of a learning community, either in their individual or collective roles. Yet ample research shows that teachers can't be prepared for all they are ever going to teach; therefore, on-the-job learning will be necessary. In transformed schools, teachers should be models of "learning how to learn" *for understanding* (a key learning goal for their students).

Ball and McDiarmid (1990) state that most prospective teachers have few opportunities in school, college, or the wider culture to come to understand the substance and nature of their subject matter. Yet Wineburg and Wilson (1988) claim that teachers' capacity to increase, deepen, or change their understanding of subject matter depends on the personal understanding of the subject matter they bring with them to the classroom.

Most learning is probably acquired from the textbook and teacher's guide used in K–12 classes. However, Ball and McDiarmid (1990) point to the problems of misrepresented disciplinary knowledge in many school textbooks:

> History texts, for example, tend to portray accounts of the past as a process of looking up information . . . . Analysis of mathematics textbooks suggests that concepts and procedures are often inadequately developed, with just one or two examples given and an emphasis on "hints and reminders" to students about what to do. . . . Similar criticisms exist of the ways in which texts misrepresent both the substance and nature of science and writing (composition). In short, learning from textbooks, although it may help to illuminate subject-matter concepts for teachers, may also contribute to the perpetuation of thin or inaccurate representations of subject matter (p. 445).

Another shortcoming of schooling today is the lack of a collective level of learning at the school site. Weick's (1976) description of educational organizations as loosely coupled is still appropriate today. Schools are still collections of one-room schoolhouses under a common roof. Goodlad (1990) observed three characteristics of teacher preparation that bear on their roles in working together:

1. There was little evidence that teachers were learning methods of inquiry.

2. There was a common teacher belief that everyone is entitled to his own opinion no matter its basis.

3. There was no sense of training for reflectivity and an understanding of why things worked, with exploration of alternative possibilities.

Goodlad (1990) and his fellow researchers have expressed a shared dismay at the paucity of intelligent, informed discussion of teacher decision making and a lack of preparation in dialogue, compromise, and problem solving. Pintrich (1990) supports Goodlad's findings. Most teachers regard research as meaningless; to them, good pedagogical practice depends only on an individual's personal experience or opinion. Joyce (1992) calls for a sociology of knowledge, where hard data and solid research bear more weight than unsubstantiated belief in school-site decision making.

Sarason (1990) offers two additional, powerful insights that have particular parallels with TQM. First, it is virtually impossible to create and sustain conditions for productive learning for students when they do not exist for teachers. Second, the system that makes or sustains such a failure in performance must be scrutinized when one concludes that almost all the people in a particular role are inadequate. Deming couldn't have said it better.

Connecting Ways of Knowing

Beginning efforts in human resource development should focus on the three overlapping facets of teachers' ways of knowing, or epistemology: (1) content knowledge, including methodology; (2) adult cognitive development—the four Systems; and (3) views and beliefs about teaching and learning (Figure 5.3).

These ways of knowing overlap in three ways. First, System 4 thinking and deep understanding in a content domain have a commonality because both call for seeing big pictures and appreciating the history and ways of knowledge development. It is probable that both Joe and Chris, the mathematics and social studies teachers mentioned earlier in this chapter, are System 4 thinkers.

Second, as the previous discussions of Systems 1 and 4 teachers show, conceptual paradigms seem to have a direct relationship with views and beliefs about teaching and learning. Large differences in the classrooms of Systems 1 and 4 teachers existed regarding the role of teacher as expert and the nature of uncertainty and conjecture.

Third, pedagogical content knowledge (knowing possible student misconceptions and appropriate analogies to connect with current student understanding) has a direct bearing on the success of a teacher (like Joe) who chooses to work as a constructivist coach.

As educators, we have a profoundly important charge—to develop the intellectual capital of students. Our understanding and use of the ways of knowing to facilitate student development are crucial. Epistemology isn't just for philosophers anymore. It is the bedrock of solid teacher professionalism. These three ways of knowing—and the areas in which they interact—are the core of an educators' job skills. They must come first in human resource development in education because they are foundational to a deeper understanding of the quality movement, the use of problem-solving tools, and the development of group process skills.

FIGURE 5.3

Overlapping Ways of Knowing

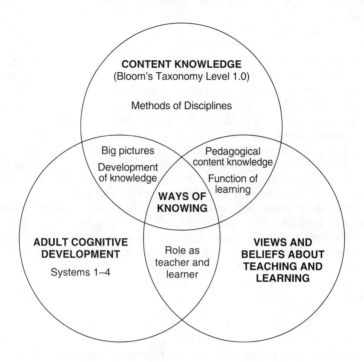

For example, the foremost TQM value is seeing that the problem is in the system and not with individuals. The ability to understand this quality value is based primarily on one's cognitive level—being able, as in System 4 thinking, to see the big picture, work on abstract problems, and consider situations from many viewpoints. Seeing problems in the system often goes beyond simple cause-and-effect thinking. It calls for systems thinking (Senge 1990) or dialectical thinking (Basseches 1984). One's cognitive, or conceptual, paradigm also has a significant bearing on work within a group, using process skills. An epistemological position that depends on experts (System 1) or views all opinions as equally valid without discerning their basis (System 3) leads to poor problem-solving skills. Senge (1990) lists the abilities of identifying, suspending, and challenging assumptions as essential for productive group work and learning. These are definitely System 4 skills.

Many of the highly touted tools of the quality method—the seven Basic Tools and seven Advanced Tools (GOAL/QPC 1989a and b) are similar to methods of knowing in subject area disciplines. Many of these tools are applications of the science process skills (Schenkat and Bat-taglini 1980). Other tools are versions of thinking and problem-solving skills taught to K–12 students: cause and effect, classification, and relationship, as well as the use of pie charts, scatter diagrams, flow charts, and histograms. The Deming Plan, Do, Study, Act (PDSA) cycle is closely tied to the model learned in teachers' methods courses for lesson design. If we are to help students see beyond the surface and understand how and why things work, we should learn the methods of our subject areas, how they relate in interdisciplinary work, and how they support quality tools. Connections should be made for students with the processes that underlie the Seven Basic and Seven Advanced Tools. Unfortunately, we may not make full use of the quality tools if we do not have the content background or in-depth knowledge that fuels the successful use of tools. Research on expert problem solving shows that success depends on richly formed cognitive structures, not the generic use of tools and techniques for problem solving.

Two other important quality values (a sense of continuous improvement and an appreciation of profound knowledge) are foreign to many people's current beliefs about learning. If we view learning as a search for the precise and correct answers from experts, we will not see learning as recursive, continually being refined, and being more deeply understood. For educators, a solid foundation in the three facets of ways of knowing is the prerequisite for an awareness of the quality movement, the use of problem-solving tools, and acquisition of group process skills.

Providing a foundation in the ways of knowing is a tremendous leadership challenge. "Ways of knowing," as a topic itself, is very ego threatening; it attacks the very core of professional existence. But we can no longer ignore this foundational area.

I have participated in rigorous efforts with teachers in exploring the ways of knowing, including an intensive five-week summer program for elementary teachers to develop a conceptual understanding of physics. In this program, teachers attended twelve hours of class per week and studied for three-and-a-half hours every day (including weekends). Teachers have found the experience growth enhancing and have asked for more (Morehouse, Battaglini, and Schenkat 1991). The old system kept teachers as prisoners in an intellectually sterile environment.

Issues in ways of knowing are systems problems. Most of us have experienced learning only from the paradigm described by Arons (1985)—the regurgitation model. As leaders, we need to keep this challenge at the forefront of our consciousness. Again, Sarason (1990) said this well: "When one concludes that almost all people in a particular role are inadequate, should one not ask what there is about the system that makes or sustains such failure in performance?" (p. 15).

We need to consider some of the fundamental human resource development tenets identified by Deming. For example, many typical personnel practices, such as ranking, evaluations, and merit pay, have negative consequences. We need to figure out ways to encourage people, not damage them. We need to strike out fear by attending to issues of job security and establishing conditions that mitigate psychological threat. We need to support educators' acting as a community of learners from a System 4 position. The National Board of Professional Teaching Standards (NBPTS 1991) offers some glimpse of what these conditions look like: professionals working at a school site focused on continuous improvement by being organized to find and solve problems and locate, invent, and experiment with different methods of instruction and school organization. (See Appendix C for a list of NBPTS proposed standards.)

In addition, we need to develop opportunities to guide rigorous growth in in-depth knowledge of subject areas and in developing a sense of constructed knowing. Tools such as Computer Supported Intentional Learning Environments (CSILE) (Scardemalia et al. 1989), designed to foster constructivist learning in students, also hold much potential for teachers. CSILE is a joint venture of the Ontario Institute for Studies in Education and Apple Computers.* The program supports *intentional learning* by providing a means for a group of learners to build a collective data base of their thoughts, which are available to all learners in the form of pictures and written notes. The system is a form of hypermedia that allows notes entered as text, drawings, graphs, and timelines to be retrieved, linked, or commented on. This learning will be time consuming and arduous, but we must offer the necessary challenge and support to aid individuals in what is a personal transformation.

Job skills enhancement is the heart of the transformation—in both schools and the workplace. Providing quality human resource development is a tremendous challenge and at the core of education's ability to support a productive economy and meaningful civic and personal lives.

---

*Apple Computers is considering plans to commercially market CSILE as MAC SCILE.

6

Quality Plans, Results, and Customer Satisfaction

s Chapter 3 states, all Deming quality values and all Baldrige criteria are interrelated: a quality product depends on quality leadership, a quality process, and quality human resource development. This chapter examines the remaining Baldrige criteria and their foundation in the thoughts of W. Edwards Deming. These criteria are strategic quality planning, information and analysis, quality and operational results, and customer focus and satisfaction (see Figure 3.1 in Chapter 3 for a flowchart showing the interrelationship of all Baldrige criteria). My discussions of these latter criteria are brief and are accompanied by this cautionary note: In the transformation of American schools, efforts directed at, say, strategic quality planning will produce scant results unless we first attend to cultivating leadership, improving our core technologies for teaching and learning, and developing our human resources (as discussed in Chapters 3–5).

Strategic Quality Planning

Strategic planning is the fashionable thing to do these days. Many schools and districts are taking their cues from business and coming up with detailed strategic plans that go into the next century. I would use caution in expending energy in strategic planning until a sense of transformation in teaching and learning is present. If strategy plans miss this sense, they will be for naught.

Deming Foundation

The Deming foundation in strategic quality planning provides a view of innovation, constancy of purpose, and the shallowness of plans based on goals without the means to accomplish them. To Deming, innovation can't thrive unless top management has declared an unshakable commitment to quality and productivity. Work on new products and services to generate new business should be undertaken five to eight years before the new product or service comes out. A company with good management will require five years to remove barriers. Some companies need ten years. Deming is opposed to numerical goals, and he emphasizes that any goal set without a viable means for accomplishing it is a charade.

Baldrige Criteria

The Baldrige criterion on strategic quality planning includes the following illustrative subcriteria:

- State the company (or school) vision for the next five years.
- Describe how quality is integrated throughout company goals.
- Describe how goals are to be deployed and indicate the sufficiency of capital expenditures.
- State specifically what is going to improve and why.
- Develop goals that are concrete, focused, integrated, and aggressive (goals that spur the organization to break the mold).
- Link quality strategic planning to the other six criteria of the Baldrige Award.

Educational Implications

The educational implications of Strategic Quality Planning are enormous; this kind of planning turns the usual budget-linked planning upside down. In quality planning, a mutual understanding of the need for innovation to transform schools must be coupled with new thinking about resource allocation and use. Today, good schools need to "retool" for human resource development and quality processes and products— for transforming our core technologies for teaching and learning. In customary practice, schools make plans based on what's available: "Here are the state and local dollars for development—what will we do?" This mindset needs to be replaced by a strategic plan with goal deployment and sufficiency of capital expenditures. The vagaries of funding for research and development (R&D) contribute to a pendulum theory of innovation. Grants only exacerbate uncertainty with a lack of constancy of purpose.

We must develop internal and external understanding of this dilemma. Businesses don't conduct R&D without some long-term financial commitment. They don't build a budget that will place money in R&D only if the salary settlement is not too high. *Here is where schools need to operate more like businesses.* However, we will appreciate this need for development only when we realize the staggering demands that face us.

Both Deming and Baldrige call for consideration of extended time frames. This long-term approach is particularly important in building high expectations throughout the curriculum. Low expectations become self-reinforcing—particularly through the tacit teacher-student contracts discussed in Chapter 4. Sometimes teachers have such low expectations for their students that meeting the new standards being developed in many subject areas seems impossible. For example, as a result of extensive K–2 language arts curriculum revision (Schenkat, Sievers, and Goplen 1991), 2nd grade students are expected to complete a story map (a type of outline) and also use story map features in their writing. These expectations exceed what is currently believed to be possible for many middle school and high school students. It is difficult for teachers to envision higher expectations when current practice has so limited and confirmed previous low expectations. In quality strategic planning, curriculum developers are challenged to lead students—and teachers—to accomplish heretofore "unreasonable" expectations.

Designing in quality in curriculums is extensive work. Typical curriculum development scenarios often include a few representative, districtwide, volunteer teachers on a time-pressured schedule. Such sessions yield few truly conceptualized outcomes; mostly they are cut and pasted with slight, if any, attention given to how these outcomes might be assessed. Generally, there is little investment in the process; and curriculum guides are delivered and shelved by teachers because the all-inclusive new textbook recommended by the "curriculum developers" *becomes* the curriculum. This process is markedly different from the designing in of quality that results from a "quality function deployment plan" (GOAL/QPC Research Committee 1991).

There is power in a deployment plan (see Chapter 7). A deployment plan gives us the ability to see the scope of what needs to be done, talk about it, and project reasonable costs and time frames. In business, quality costs—but it pays off in the reduction of inspection, warranties, and rework. In schools, as well, building in quality has its costs, but there are also prospects of huge savings in education (Schenkat 1988). Consider the costs of compensatory programs such as Chapter 1 and special education, retention, and assessment expenses. For instance, it is estimated that each student consumes 100 hours per year in test-taking activities (Paris, Lawton, Turner, and Roth 1991) at an approximated cost for all U.S. students of $0.5 *billion* annually (Smith 1991). Currently, creativity in uses of funding is mired in the suboptimization of competing educational "profit centers," such as Chapter 1, special education, remedial education, and regular education. As Deming would suggest, we need to remove barriers and strike out fear if we are to engage in creative problem solving. In addition, perhaps communities could be persuaded to underwrite the cost of the development of quality in schools. Pledges of long-term sufficiency may come if campaigns were supported and led by business leaders who value the quality transformation in their organizations.

Information and Analysis

In discussions of Total Quality Management, many people start to quake at the thought that they might, after all, have to *really* use statistics. Mention the words *variation* and *data*, and people's eyes start to glaze. But obtaining information and analyzing it go far beyond statistical charts and graphs. Using information and analysis involves understanding how and why something works and how to improve the process. It has to do with observation, measurement, and deep understanding of the process. Baldrige emphasizes "benchmarking," which is observing successful practices at other organizations and applying what you learn to your own organization.

Deming Foundation

The Deming foundation in information and analysis offers insights into benchmarking, inspection, and the reality of uncertainty gained from measurement. Deming would endorse the concept of benchmarking, which provides a deep understanding of why something is working and encourages the adaptation of those beneficial elements and principles to the new setting. However, he is cautious of copying procedures and processes without full understanding of the process, which is what is commonly happening today in benchmarking. Deming (1992) also admonishes:

> Cease dependence on mass inspection; you cannot inspect in quality. Once a process is in control, use statistical process control procedures occasionally to ensure the process is not regressing. Some of the most important areas are unknown or unknowable so do not be caught up in an excessive mania to count and measure (p. 42).

Baldrige Criteria

The Baldrige criterion on information and analysis includes the following helpful guidelines, or subcriteria:

• Describe the process of benchmarking from the best competing companies.

• Know the processes used in the benchmarking process; don't copy based on results.

• Determine if the data collected are useful and are being used; is there fact-based management relying on hard data?

• Determine if the data drive solutions and if the company is getting better in a variety of areas.

• Describe how the data influence company goals.

• Determine if there is a systematic evaluation of data-collection procedures.

Educational Implications

The educational implications of the Baldrige Information and Analysis criterion include many concrete ways to improve our learning environments. Gathering information and analyzing it involves observing and understanding the principles behind what other, successful organizations are doing (benchmarking), questioning what is worth measuring, aggregating and disaggregating data, and considering the needs (and contributions) of parents.

Benchmarking. Collecting and using information about another organization's practices and performance can be an antidote to the limited expectations often set for students as learners. Garvin (1991) points out:

> Truly excellent companies use benchmarking as a catalyst and enabler of change, a learning process rather than a score card. They scan the world widely for organizations that are skilled at what they do, visit them to gain a better understanding of their processes and ways of working, and use the findings to stretch their imaginations and develop new ways of operating (p. 91).

Several researchers have provided examples of results and processes that can be used as benchmarks:

• Roth studied meaning making in eighteen middle school students who used (1) conventional science textbooks and (2) a prototype text designed for conceptual change. While using two commercial science textbooks, less than 10 percent of the students demonstrated conceptual change. In the prototype reading material, 84 percent of the students demonstrated an understanding reflecting conceptual change. This group of 7th graders included two students with 3.4 and 5.6 grade equivalent reading scores (Anderson and Roth 1989). This work sets a performance benchmark: even typically lower-ability students can read for conceptual change. This study describes the nature of reading material that prompts conceptual change.

• Wineburg (1991) found that even gifted high school students tend to appreciate blandly written history texts that just give the facts. Expert historians, however, can read texts to gain insight into the interaction of content background and historical thinking while making meaning in passages. This research gives us a glimpse of the processes that need to be modeled for students to obtain a deep understanding of history.

• Sambs and Schenkat (1987) demonstrated that even low-quartile readers at the end of a 1st grade reading intervention could reach the ceiling on a conventional word attack measure (the Woodcock Johnson). There was a mean scoring of 3.3 grade equivalent for an effect size of 1.3 (Slavin 1989). These findings set high expectations for low-ability students, who seldom attain automaticity in word recognition in traditional reading instruction (Woodward and Schenkat 1989). This lack of automaticity often leads to special education placement.

• Other researchers have also obtained results that show the effects of setting high expectations. High school students with learning disabilities were mainstreamed for a higher-order thinking intervention in science. On a chemistry test that required applying concepts such as bonding, equilibrium, energy of activation, atomic structure, and organic compounds, the students did not differ significantly from control students in an advanced placement chemistry course (Hofmeister, Engelmann, and Carnine 1989). Also, assessment scores for skills in argument, construction, and critiquing for high school students with mild disabilities were as high as or higher than scores of high school students in an honors English class and college students enrolled in a teacher certification program (Grossen and Carnine 1990).

High expectations for learners at all levels of ability are vitally important. Sarason (1990) describes the prevailing mindset:

> Generally speaking, in and out of the classroom, we underestimate the capability of children to pursue answers on their own. We respond as if they are irresponsible in this regard, and we usually end up proving the self-fulfilling prophecy (p. 91).

In the old paradigm, excuses were offered for not meeting high expectations. In a TQM approach, those expectations can be met by understanding and planning for the employment of the state of the art in teaching and learning strategies. Rather than lengthening the school year, we need to ensure optimal use of research-validated practices (Gilhool, Laski, and Gold 1987).

Champions of benchmarking in the corporate world, such as American Express, with their billing processes, and L.L. Bean, with their processes of distribution, could be useful to education in illustrating how processes have been drastically improved. The expression "break the mold" comes from benchmarking, as what seem like unattainable results are obtained. In furthering the relationship and understanding between businesses and schools, people in both types of organizations can share locally exemplary results and performance.

Determining What's Worth Measuring. We can attach numerical values to "learning." Achievement test batteries have existed for the past four decades; but we need to be cautious about using numbers to validate performance. Roth (1992) recently described the outcomes of related learning for the students of three teachers working in a highly interdependent learning community. Although their science, social studies, and language arts curriculum were not integrated and planned in the traditional sense, 5th grade students revealed an understanding of big themes in an end-of-the-year interview with teachers. It is easy to convert grade books to control charts, but are such data worth charting? Those results are not as important as the study and improvement action taken in the PDSA cycle. For customer satisfaction, it is better to enhance a school's capacity for documentation of true student performance. Alverno College uses a cadre of trained community assessors to validate student competence in performance settings. Several midwestern K–12 districts are working with Alverno to replicate this assessment system for use with their students.

Aggregating and Disaggregating Data. Data sources can be much more meaningful if they are integrated and the results disaggregated. Figure 6.1 shows how such data can be used to make decisions about placement of students in certain classes. In this chart, a 2nd grade group of 346 students is sorted by placement in compensatory education, reading fluency scores in four quartiles, achievement test comprehension measures, and information on second-attempt mastery. Such an integrated data set allows for raising numerous questions and inferences. For example, in category A, should the twelve students in Chapter 1 be priorities for next year? How much growth occurred for these twelve students during the school year? Five of the twelve students in quartile 1 who were not in Compensatory Education were not in Chapter 1 schools; are their needs being met? Using information in this manner suggests that integrating information creates a more useful reporting process that considers all students in one report. This approach is superior to different accounting reports currently used in regular education, Chapter 1, and in special education programs.

Parent Learning and Relearning. Facilitating the educational transformation involves making new learning available to both students and parents. A community premium should be placed on growth and relearning at all levels, including corporate and school district leaders and parents. A father with a doctoral degree was recently discussing with me the in-depth learning his son was experiencing in a high school literature class. The father expressed a yearning to develop a deeper appreciation of literature—and in the process certainly modeled an openness to learning for his son. This new ethic of learning is the foundation of TQM at its most profound level.

Quality and Operational Results

The history of U.S. educational reforms is full of failed efforts and stalled innovations—often because results are slow in coming and people lose patience. Quality results take time—measured in years, not months, semesters, or quarters. Educators engaged in recent efforts at restructuring schools have learned this:

> Change takes time, and big changes take a long time. Deep shifts in the pattern of a school take time to be visualized, practiced, and integrated into the whole . . . . [The] process is slow, and it must be

nurtured with knowledge, commitment, and resources (Berreth, Crawford, Curran, and Nicklas 1992, p. 13).

Deming quality values and Baldrige criteria offer invaluable guidance in achieving quality results. In business terms, results are profits; in education, the results are intrinsically motivated, lifelong learners.

Deming Foundation

The Deming foundation in TQM causes us to realize the difficulty in quantifying gains in one year to show the investment benefits from quality programs. Deming also stresses that profits follow from doing quality work. This is a real mindshift. Quality practices are not embraced to produce higher profits; but when the focus is on doing better, profits are the natural result.

Baldrige Criteria

The Baldrige category of quality and operational results includes the following helpful subcriteria:

• Describe operational results in productivity, efficiency, effectiveness, and cost.

• Show results in data tracked to information and analysis criteria.

• Show meaningful trends over three to ten years in industry comparisons.

• Show a relationship between quality results and customer satisfaction.

• Prove that quality is not caused by serendipity.

• Show results data regarding improvements in business support processes and suppliers.

Educational Implications

The educational implications of quality results apply well to issues of educational equity when mastery is expected of all students. Deming's adamancy against ranking also has important implications for today's practices. With an emphasis on quality results, schools, businesses, and other organizations begin to have a common yardstick for performance—how they have deployed quality throughout the organization and with what results. Educational expectations now apply to all learners. Formerly, the range of achievement levels grew wider the longer that students stayed in school. Today we expect a mastery approach, ensuring that all students succeed. This reflects not only an ideal of equity, but also a realization that the workplace cannot absorb workers without skills.

From Jenkins, Stein, and Osborn's (1981) observations of the effectiveness of reading comprehension instructional material, we can infer that several factors play a role in reading comprehension achievement. Jenkins notes, "A student's ability to comprehend a text may have little

FIGURE 6.1

Data for Decision Making About a District's 2nd Grade

Not in Compensatory Education

Category	Qtr. 1	Qtr. 2	Qtr. 3	Qtr. 4
* less than 75 w.p.m. * 20 or less on SAT * not mastering second reading A	12			
* less than 75 w.p.m. * 20 or less on SAT * mastery second reading B	18	2		
* 75–95 w.p.m. * 20 or less on SAT C		17	3	
* +95 w.p.m. * 20 or less on SAT * mastery second reading D			6	3
* less than 75 w.p.m. * +21 on SAT * more than 95 w.p.m. on second reading E	19			
* less than 75 w.p.m. * +21 on SAT * less than 95 w.p.m. on second reading F	8			
In Compensatory Education G				
* +21 on SAT * more than 75 w.p.m. on first reading (est.) H		53	77	83
Total				

Note: Qtr. 1, Qtr. 2, and so forth refer to students' scores (in quartiles) on a reading fluency test; LD = classes for students with learning

In Compensatory Education

Chapt. 1 Qtr. 1	Chapt. 1 Qtr. 2	LD Qtr. 1	LD Qtr. 2	Sp. Ed. Qtr. 1	Total
12		1			25
5		3		1	29
	3				23
			1		10
5		1		1	26
3					11
7		2			9
					213
					346

disabilities; Sp. Ed. = other special education classes; SAT = Stanford Achievement Test; w.p.m. = words per minute read.

to do with the comprehension prescribed in most commercial reading programs" (p. 29). Rather, many results have come from children's self-teaching abilities.

Disaggregating data gives a much clearer picture of the full range of learners coming to mastery. We should be looking at trends over three to ten years, and we can do this best by using absolute standards on performance-based tests. It will take time to have quality measures of quality results. The National Board of Professional Teaching Standards (1991) is grappling with many assessment issues (see Appendix C). Sharing quality standards could be as beneficial as benchmarking processes in industry.

Deming is adamantly against ranking because of its demoralizing effects and the obvious result that 50 percent will always be below average. Currently, standardized achievement tests are still much in vogue. Often they do not allow for long-term comparisons because test forms vary or different editions have different norming groups. In addition to showing quality results for students, other measures should be developed to show improvements in dealing with "suppliers" (parents) and other more businesslike processes, such as phone responsiveness and so forth.

A Deming approach focuses on quality first; profits follow quality. This concept has interesting implications for education. In the past, comparisons between business and education weren't made because schools weren't working for profit. Now the degree of TQM implementation should be the basis for comparison between profit and nonprofit organizations. This could prove to be an interesting topic for conversation with community leaders from all different sectors.

Customer Focus and Satisfaction

As mentioned in Chapter 4, educators on a TQM journey often spend too much time asking "Who is the customer?"—and too little time asking, "Why has the educational establishment been so unsuccessful in the attainment of the core outcomes most agree upon?" In schools, our customers are not only the students, but the entire community, including the future workplaces of our students. And how can we conduct a customer survey of future bosses, supervisors, and coworkers? This is where creativity, imagination, innovation, and a deep understanding of future needs are essential.

Deming Foundation

The Deming foundation in customer satisfaction provides insights into this popular quality area. Deming says the customer is the most important part of the extended process. Deming also believes in a personal ethic of wanting to do the best job for the satisfaction of doing it. Although customers are the most important part of the extended process, Deming is cognizant that customers seldom know what they need beyond a three-year time frame. Thus, product development for customers comes from imagination and knowledge of customers' needs. Deming has estimated that perhaps only one-eighth of dissatisfied customers voice a complaint; the balance just go elsewhere to do business.

Baldrige Criteria

The Baldrige customer focus and satisfaction criterion includes the following illustrative subcriteria:

• Describe how to determine the most important factors in maintaining and building relationships with customers and implement development plans.

• Describe how data on customers is aggregated and used throughout the company for action.

• Document the frequency of contacts to build relationships.

• Set service standards for timeliness, courtesy, efficiency, and thoroughness (compare this with competitors).

• Segment different customers and their needs, looking beyond current customers to those being lost and being pursued.

• Describe how employees in the front line are empowered to solve customer problems and how everyone beyond the front line is informed of customer needs.

• Describe the ease customers have in offering complaints and the nature of commitments and warranties to customers.

• Describe how the company provides information to customers for realistic expectations.

• Examine customer behavior—not just their opinions; thinking about things that make them happy and delighted—even anticipating things the customers don't know about themselves.

• Describe the process for determining customer wants in the future.

Educational Implications

The educational implications of Customer Focus and Satisfaction provide insights into student evaluation, school choice, and the bases for parent judgment of schools. Customer satisfaction in education is a tricky area. There is a great discrepancy between espoused principles and practice. Cardinal Newman's description of the well-educated person as one who is able to "see things as they are, to go right to the point, to disentangle a skein of thought, to detect what is sophisticated, and to discard what is irrelevant" (Newman 1973) exemplifies society's ability to articulate the product (see Chapter 4 for more of Newman's thoughts about education). Yet education has continued to produce graduates who fit well into the hierarchical and traditionally managed business world, but are poorly equipped for the challenges of transformed work-places required today.

The current system works in such a way that often the very processes and products that would serve the learner best are considered unsatisfactory. A student who is a System 1, or "black-and-white," thinker is frustrated by a teacher who doesn't tell the answers.

A challenging teacher may only be fully appreciated years later, as Deming (1992) related from a New York University finding. A survey conducted with graduates a decade after they left the university sought their perceptions about the most influential faculty members in the students' development. The survey results revealed that no faculty member who won a teacher-of-the-year award was rated ten years later as "influential."

Deming frequently asks managers who blame workers for lack of productivity and quality, "But how can they know?" The same question applies in education: "How can the students know?" Customer satisfaction must be guided by our profound knowledge of full human development. The challenge relates to our own personal level of development. Schools, as learning organizations, must focus on personal mastery—for teachers as well as students (Senge 1990). Teachers' personal growth will increase their ability to develop and sustain student learning environments that nurture the students' full development.

Attaining customer satisfaction is further complicated by subtle differences in parental expectations, new work force expectations, and variations in classroom teachers. The ultimate in customer satisfaction appears to be *school choice*—allowing parents and students to select schools. Baumrind's (1971, 1987) research views parental control on a continuum: at one extreme, laissez-faire or permissive parents who exert little or no effort to control; at the other extreme, authoritarian parents who exert and maintain control over their child's decision making. The middle ground is authoritative parents who provide explanations for their firm but flexible limits on children. They discuss their standards, teach their child how to meet them, and value behavior that is monitored by self-discipline and self-control. This position seems to bear the closest resemblance to the National Governors' Association (1988) description of self-regulated workers, who have the ability "to communicate complex ideas, to analyze and solve complex problems, to identify order and find direction in an ambiguous environment, and to think and reason abstractly" (see Chapter 1). However, as McCaslin and Good (1992) point out, "It does not take a great deal of imagination to predict how the differing parental management styles would manifest themselves in school selections for children if a voucher system were instituted" (p. 12).

Another issue in customer satisfaction is the belief that schools need to return to the *basics of the good old days*. Goodlad's (1983) descriptions of schools were appropriate a generation ago when there was less variation from suppliers (many more stable two-parent homes) and no expectation of mastery results for *all* students. It is a myth to say that we have good schools that are getting better. According to Deming (1992), schools in their current configurations serve as a major force for destruction of self-esteem. Ironically, we dabble with courses and units on self-esteem within a system currently configured to destroy it. In overcoming the "good old days" myth, discussion about actual experiences in learning could be helpful. A realization that our schooling was inadequate might be caused by reflecting on questions like: How did we learn? How confident were we in sharing assumptions or, for that matter, even recognizing them? How open were we? How did we deal with ambiguity?

As I listened to leaders at one company talk about workplace empowerment, I heard many common themes stressing that workers need more trust in themselves as learners and thinkers, and they need confidence that their ideas have as much merit as those of the boss and the outside experts. The leaders suggested that old ways of schooling have done much to limit employee confidence.

Business leaders want outcomes such as those proposed in SCANS or by the National Governors' Association. Baldrige criteria suggest describing how the company provides information to customers so that their expectations are realistic. If the anticipated outcomes are seeing patterns to solve problems, synthesizing disparate information, identifying problems, and constructing solutions, then business must understand the magnitude of retooling and change necessary in education. There can be no quick fixes. Applying TQM thinking, such as cause-and-effect diagrams, profound knowledge, and deployment, should help make this clear.

We have discussed some of the subtler aspects of customer satisfaction. At a more tangible level, parents appreciate a sense that their opinions matter, as well as open communication with teachers, a responsive principal, and the knowledge that their children are known at the school site.

Finally, in relation to the "customer at large" in a total community system, I estimate that at least 75 percent of the information citizens obtain about the school system is conveyed through local newspapers. School leaders should work with the media to cover school news in the context of the big picture and with a sense of the underlying quality values undergirding decisions.

7

Deployment Planning

The preceding chapters have established the foundation for a plan to transform education, using background on the philosophy and quality values of W. Edwards Deming and the seven Baldrige National Quality Award criteria. In Chapters 3–6, I also related the implications of these ideas and processes for your school district and education in general (see Figure 3.2 and Appendix A for concrete applications of TQM principles in education, listed under the Baldrige criteria). I assume that you are convinced of the necessity of developing quality in education, but have very few resources currently allocated for TQM. Further, I assume that you appreciate the rigor and challenge of this task. According to Sarason (1990), changing a system is not for the conceptually and interpersonally fainthearted. This chapter presents a deployment plan with a long-range view; it supports the risk-taker, includes the community, and builds on our state of the art—for leaders, for teachers, and for students and their families.

Figure 7.1 shows a deployment planning matrix for transformed schools: starting a quality program, operating a beginning quality program, and sustaining a total quality program. Each of these time periods lasts from one to four years; the total effort could take from five to ten years. The points listed give a sense of the possible activities or results that could occur. For example, under the Baldrige criterion Leadership for Quality, education leaders who are starting a quality program would develop links with other community efforts to implement TQM.

Each item in the matrix offers some insight into the many specifics that can undergird a TQM vision. Also, each of the time frames has a simultaneous occurrence of activities in the major Baldrige criteria areas. Although all seven areas are mentioned, the degree of effort in all areas will not be the same. Their ordering on the matrix from left to right represents my sense of their importance in transforming American schools.

The first column is leadership; quality transformation is not something that can be delegated. This column shows that leaders must understand the application of TQM to two somewhat distinct new paradigms: (1) operating an organization based on quality values and (2) the new practice of constructivist learning. These paradigms reflect the dual nature of the TQM challenge in education. Leadership is the key to bringing education, in Deming's terms, out of the crisis.

The second column relates to products and services—the technology of teaching and learning what education is about. There needs to be clarity throughout the organization regarding the learning process.

Success in the quality process heavily depends on the development of human resources (Column 3). Education has to address both organizational shifts based on quality values and new practices in teaching and learning (our core technologies). Without attention to the profound changes that humans have to make in operating schools, there is little sense in attending to the other criteria—strategic quality planning, information and analysis, quality results, and customer satisfaction. However, if we are serious about human resource development, then it is critical to develop a plan for sufficient resource allocation to support organization change (Column 4, Strategic Quality Planning).

The remaining criteria are important, but attending to them without extensive work in Columns 1–3 will be futile. These remaining three criteria represent 56 percent of the Baldrige points; and one might be tempted to think this is where effort should be directed if this is where point allocations come from. I would advise against getting caught up in numerical scoring, however, especially in the early years.

Starting a Quality Program

Personal leadership and time commitment are essential to the success of TQM in transforming schools. Business leaders starting a quality program could spend four full days at an introductory Deming Seminar just to begin learning about a new paradigm of leadership. The implications for education require even more of a learning commitment. Support groups of educators and other business leaders can be very valuable. If community quality councils exist (Community Quality Coalition), a school leader can easily find allies on the quality journey.

An understanding of constructivism and learning for conceptual change are the two most important foundations for quality processes and products in education. District activities should complement each other as a coordinated, extended process is sought. The quality movement has been misused to increase productivity and reduce the work force. In orienting educators to TQM, integrity suggests that we use it to guarantee employment. Fear should be driven out, and there should be no perception that TQM is being used to eliminate jobs of currently employed school staff.

There should be some attempt to coordinate efforts in TQM training throughout the community. Much mutual understanding can be gained

FIGURE 7.1

Deployment Planning Matrix for Transformed Schools

Stage	Leadership for Quality	Assurance of Product and Service Quality	Human Resource Development and Management
Starting a Quality Program	• Learn the quality values and their implications for education • Develop personal support mechanisms • Link to broad-based community movement focused on TQM done thoughtfully	• Understand constructivism and learning for conceptual change • Synthesize ongoing district efforts	• Guarantee that no jobs will be lost from TQM (drive out fear) • Orient all employees to quality values through introductory program (consider joint training with other local firms) • Invest heavily in leaders and in envisioning learning communities
Operating a Beginning Quality Program	• Lead consistently day to day; model learning with staff; see things getting better • Push for 14 points daily in obvious way by top management • Apply TQM through a trained middle management group (principals) • Communicate quality values to the public	• Design in quality in curriculum development processes • Begin working with suppliers • Build in mechanism of continuous improvement (time issues, action research, quality tools)	• Attain intended implementation through staff development • Reconsider existing evaluation practices • Foster professionalism set forth in NBPTS
Sustaining a Quality Program	• See an integration of quality in all major decisions • Sense a personal transformation	• Change naturally to an interdisciplinary curriculum • Shift the ways schools provide learning	• Improve continually in allocation of human effort • Unleash optimal motivation • Convey symbolically that employees are the district's most competitive asset

Strategic Quality Plan	Information and Analysis	Quality and Operational Results	Customer Focus and Satisfaction
• Keep communication focused on long-term support and constancy of purpose • Develop support for long-range budget to support quality initiative	• Benchmark on some quality practices in community • Develop measures to sense community support	• Begin discussion on needs for *all* to learn in new paradigm (moving away from normal curve of learning)	• Conduct community dialogue regarding new demands for work, civic, and personal life • Discuss distinction between information accumulation and understanding
• Secure funding for next 5–7 years related to employee leaning needs • Link all facets of quality cohesively	• Benchmark to set high standards academically • Base decisions on data • Cease dependence on mass inspection	• Begin tracking costs that relate to the cost of inspection	• Work with community to accommodate new learning schedules • Look deeply at student growth, not just their opinions • Be responsive in solving problems (phones, voice mail)
• Carry out long-term design projects for 5–8 years with solid staff commitment • Scan futures for needed paradigm shifts	• Determine if data drive decisions and if schools are getting better in a variety of areas	• Show consistent trends in data collection • Spend fewer dollars in rework (compensatory education programs, costs of failure, etc.)	• Establish an ongoing process to determine future needs • See that community is delighted

Note: TQM = Total Quality Management; NBPTS = National Board of Professional Teaching Standards.

from joint awareness training with other local organizations, such as factories, medical facilities, and government agencies. Staff development leaders must begin the careful work needed if schools are to become learning communities.

Constancy of purpose is the watchword, as the need for strategic planning with accompanying funding becomes a reality. Benchmarking on some quality practices of other well-regarded local businesses can be an easy way to begin the start-up phase of TQM. Assessing community awareness of the transformation can also be helpful. Today, people are from the understanding that *all* can learn challenging outcomes (Resnick and Resnick 1991)—that we don't have to accept the "normal" learning curve, where more than half fail to learn even at today's current low levels. Also, as issues in customer satisfaction are considered, one of the most difficult tasks is developing community appreciation of a new learning paradigm that focuses on understanding, not just accumulation of information.

In beginning a quality program, the interrelated issues of leadership and human resource development are the most critical. However, efforts in all other areas are also necessary.

Operating a Beginning Quality Plan

Leadership in this phase is again central. "Walking the talk" is imperative. Staff members need to see things getting better because of TQM. This process will probably come most directly from middle managers (mostly principals) embracing TQM; however, this will likely be a challenging area. Staff members can also see things getting better as efforts are made to design in quality in curriculum development. Because teachers have varying conceptual paradigms with markedly different expectations, the process won't always run smoothly. (See Glickman's [1986] model, "Levels of Teacher Thought.) Mechanisms must be built for continuous improvement. Critical here is building a workday schedule to honor teacher professionalism so there is time to work on continuous improvement. Things can also get better by diligent effort in working with suppliers (parents).

As new curriculum is developed, it is critical to consider the rigorous staff development and coaching necessary to ensure intended implementation. The National Board of Professional Teacher Standards (NBPTS) is a useful benchmark for teacher professionalism (see Appendix C). The practices of developing learning communities and encouraging teacher reflection are also salient in the NBPTS. Recalling why Deming is adamantly against current rating systems in personnel policies, we should carefully reconsider existing evaluation processes.

Because of the foundation set for long-term planning, schools and districts should secure funding to plan for comprehensive staff and curriculum development, in five- to seven-year time frames. All facets in the district that relate to TQM will be cohesively linked. Benchmarks set in performance standards will become common, as will data-based decision making; and mass inspection by standardized tests will become less common. Cost data, as one form of quality results, will show that prevention pays. Savings will come from less mass inspection, less failure, and less consequent rework.

Quality results will build customer satisfaction so that parents accept altered schedules, where teachers spend less time lecturing students—and *all* students do higher-level independent and team work. Customer satisfaction cannot be gleaned from simple paper-and-pencil attitudinal surveys alone, but should be guided by many forms of evidence that show student cognitive and social development.

Sustaining a Quality Program

Leadership is best evidenced when quality is integrated into all major decisions and leaders talk of personal transformation. Moreover, these transformations are evident to other people, as leaders model growth and show the changes they have undergone. The integration of quality values into the organization could be indicated by the promotion of individuals who espouse and practice quality and a budgeting process reflecting dollars earmarked for quality.

The quality of meaningfully integrated curriculums, one of the measures of product quality, will increase as teachers grow personally in a deeper understanding of the power of learning communities and the richness of disciplines. The more we value and nurture cognitively sophisticated thinking (the System 4 level of adult cognitive development, as described in Chapter 5), the more we can build higher levels of learning into the curriculum—to allow for multiple perspectives, ambiguity, and system and dialectical thinking. With these changes, the nature of the teaching and learning process will also be open to modification, as shown in Figure 3.2. Until teachers are ready, attempts at this integration will result only in contrived efforts.

In the current paradigm, school board actions and politics generally capture the lion's share of school district news. Rarely is the community informed about its teachers—or that educators' talents are the backbone of the district. An organization subscribing to quality values will be investing heavily in human development. The fact that teachers are the most valued asset must be continually conveyed to the public. In addition, we need flexibility for decision makers to best decide on the optimal use of human talent. In the current paradigm, contracts and certifications often hamper this flexibility. In applications of TQM to education, the need for flexibility applies most directly to site-based management. Removal of barriers should aid in unleashing optimal motivation.

Long-range strategic quality plans, with five- to eight-year time frames, reflect a constancy of purpose that will support staff confidence in the seriousness of change efforts. Futures scanning will focus on needed paradigm shifts in curriculum and delivery, thus serving as a hedge on continuous improvement of strategies that might have outlived their usefulness. To use an analogy from the automobile world, we might be trying to improve fuel efficiency of gasoline engines long after batteries, or solar power, or some other future sources of power become available. We don't want to miss a potential breakthrough. In schools today, a great deal of achievement and attendance data is collected, but little is used in systematic decision making. By the sustaining phase of a quality program, evidence would reveal that data drive decisions and trends show that things are getting better. At a minimum, this calls for consistency in data collection so that comparability is possible. By this final stage, there should be solid data to prove that in schools and districts that adopt TQM, fewer funds have to be spent in rework, such as retention, compensatory programs, special education, and other such programs. Less rework spending—this has been a common finding in most industries on a quality journey.

The deployment plan, with all its coordination for quality, should keep customers—students, parents, business, and the community—informed and appreciative of the complex challenges that educators face. As people in the community become aware of other quality efforts in business and government, they should have a heightened awareness and *delight* in the efforts undertaken by educators.

Conclusion:
Ways of Knowing

Thomas Jefferson and John Dewey both looked beyond economic necessity when they called for the full development of American citizens. Economically, however, agrarian and industrial societies needed few well-educated people. In fact, it has been suggested that too many fully developed individuals are obstacles in an industrial society (Goodlad 1979). The need today for the development of intellectual capital, or human resource development, is not voiced because we are at the peak of the human potential movement. Rather, we hear calls for higher-order learning because people who possess these skills are necessary for our economic survival in an increasingly complex and competitive technological world. In the future, the prosperity of countries will depend on their ability to create value through people, not by a mere husbanding of resources and technologies.

Quality, as explained by W. Edwards Deming, at a deep level of understanding and application, can begin to serve as a vehicle for any organization to create value through people. Quality isn't a quick fix—the simple application of Deming's famous fourteen points. The quick fix is a common American mindset, as reflected in the criticism that TQM is already receiving. *Newsweek* recently conveyed in a headline, "Faced with Hard Times, Business Sours on Total Quality Management" (Mathews and Katel 1992). *Human Resource Magazine* (Liebman 1992) begins a story, "After several hundred thousand dollars and 18 months of analysis, meetings, and recommendations, a midwest company suspended its TQM efforts. Its CEO actively supported the process . . . yet concluded that he had missed the boat."

Rather than seeing TQM as a quick fix, I suggest that there is much depth in TQM. The analysis in Chapter 1, as summarized in Figure 1.10, compares the transformations necessary in both workplaces and schools, and contrasts that many-faceted paradigm shift with customary practices. Here, I reemphasize that Deming's views on quality are really his personal *way of knowing*, or epistemology (a branch of philosophy studying knowing). More important than the fourteen points is a realization that Deming's way of knowing is based on his knowledge of theories of systems, variation, knowledge, and psychology. He is truly a model for educators as they personally understand their own ways of knowing. Personal leadership transformation (Stayer 1990) will need to precede organizational transformation. We need to become more like Deming in developing and consistently using our own ways of knowing.

In the following passage, Persig (1974) speaks of a journey that is akin to the deeper understanding of quality:

> I want to talk about another high country now in the world of thought, which in some ways, for me at least, seems to parallel or produce feelings similar to this, and call it the high country of the mind. If all of human knowledge, everything that is known, is believed to be an enormous hierarchical structure, then the high country of the mind is found at the upper-most reaches of this structure in the most general and abstract considerations of all.

> Few people travel here. In the high country of the mind one has to become adjusted to the thinner air of uncertainty . . . . Many trails through these high ranges have been made and forgotten since the beginning of time (pp. 111–112).

For the *creation of value through people* that our new economy calls for, leaders must first become comfortable in the high country of the mind. Next, we need to lead expeditions into these peaks. Finally, we need to discover ways for large groups to comfortably live in this new environment. America's educators *should* play a critical role in this exploration. The transformed school environment *should be* a series of experiences that give the learner comfort in this new terrain.

Given the *shoulds*, we also have to realize the stark realities. Findings presented in Chapter 5 indicate massive encampments of educators on the plains with almost no scouting into the high country. Generally, the high country exploration that does take place isn't officially sanctioned. Consequently, we find:

1. Educators have seldom learned beyond facts; thus deep understanding is often absent. This has a direct bearing on skills in curriculum design, explanation for new student learnings, and attributions when students fail. Few experiences are available to give students confidence in the new terrain.

2. Educators are likely to be System 1 thinkers, using a way of knowing that works well on the plains. They are unlikely to realize the limits of the System 1 paradigm, which may allow for using the words of System 4 without any congruence between words and actions. Perhaps this is why Deming asserts that wisdom, which he defines as the application of knowledge through philosophy or the correspondence of words and actions, is rare.

3. Educators have few ways of learning. Little evidence exists that teachers have the job skills or predispositions to act as a learning community in either their individual or collective roles. Thus teachers

currently don't have the skills that easily foster a transition into mountain climbing. Activities like school-based management and site-based decision making may make life better on the plains, but they probably will not get educators into the mountains.

These stark realities set a challenging task for educational leaders who can see the need for schools to create comfort in the high country of the mind. The deployment matrix shown in Figure 7.1 (pages 82–83) offers some considerations for the educational leader embarking on the quality journey. Central to success on this journey is the leadership transformation from an old, comfortable management paradigm; a realization of the need for dramatically different core technologies in education; and the careful work in human resource development. The leader truly has a developmental challenge to overcome customary practices, because the sincere and committed efforts of today's educators are not creating the type of learners needed for the future. In meeting the developmental challenge, the National Board of Professional Teaching Standards (1991) offers a set of world-class standards that seem to prepare educators well for the high country of the mind (see Appendix C). Several respected educators (Wiggins 1991, Wilson and Wineburg in press) have suggested it would be best for encampments, not individuals, to attain the standards. The leader's task is to create systems that allow for this growth at the school site.

School leaders can be aided on their quality journey by finding fellow travelers to the high country—both educators and leaders from other organizations in all sectors of the community. Figure 8.1 contrasts characteristics of fellow travelers on the journey. Good, solid companions can offer much support, whereas ill-prepared companions may greatly hamper your progress on the journey.

FIGURE 8.1

Selecting a TQM Fellow Traveler

The Quality Journey	Solid Companions	Ill-Prepared Companions
Time Frames	To do well, we might start a settlement in 8–10 years.	If we really kick butt, we can be going in 2 years.
Ways to Accomplish	I'm going to really have to rethink how I lead.	We're going to buy the "X" Program—I hear it's great.
Measuring Progress	We won't even be able to measure some of the most difficult stuff.	We will have data on everything.
Satisfying Customers	Customers don't always know what they need.	We'll give the customers what they say they want.

TQM, like any other innovation, can be undertaken for its own sake when it's in vogue or because it's suggested by business leaders. But lukewarm attempts will fail. The leader must have a deep-seated belief that life on the plains will lead to extinction and that it is the job of leaders to lead their people out of the crisis. This passionate conviction will give leaders the courage to lead the expeditions in the high country. Although this may be a tough course, it certainly is not void of pleasure and satisfaction. Many of the high country experiences that are present at birth—curiosity, joy in learning, intrinsic motivation—atrophy during life on the plains. Restoring these qualities in people and organizations can be satisfying.

It sounds heady that we should live in the high country of the mind. But this is the foundation for the TQM movement. TQM isn't a rote recipe. Rather, it is based on individual understanding and application of a profound knowledge. TQM exists in an environment where theory guides action; where there is a correspondence between words and actions—in other words, wisdom. Schools need to become centers of wisdom in this new age, ensuring that students graduate with more than heads full of inert facts. As educational leaders, we need a vision of the capacity of TQM in its many facets that leads to the transformation of our schools. Without this vision, we will stay living on the plains in an increasingly hostile environment.

References

Alverno College. (November 1990). "Expected Learning Outcomes." Paper presented at a visitation day, Alverno College, Milwaukee, Wisconsin.

Anderson, C. (1987). "Strategic Teaching in Science." In *Strategic Teaching and Learning: Cognitive Instruction in the Content Areas*, edited by B.F. Jones, A.S. Palincsar, D.S. Ogle, and E.G. Carr. Alexandria, Va.: ASCD.

Anderson, C.W., and K.J. Roth. (1989). "Teaching for Meaningful and Self-Regulated Learning of Science." In *Advances in Research on Teaching*, edited by J. Brophy. Greenwich, Conn.: JAI Press, Inc.

Apple Computer, Inc. (1992). *Newton Technology*. Cupertino, Calif.: Apple Computer, Inc.

Arons, A. (1985). "Critical Thinking and the Baccalaureate Curriculum." *Liberal Education* 71, 2: 141–157.

Ball, D.L. (1990). "The Mathematical Understandings That Prospective Teachers Bring to Teacher Education." *Elementary School Journal* 90: 449–460.

Ball, D.L. (1988). "Knowledge and Reasoning in Mathematical Pedagogy: Examining What Prospective Teaching Bring to Teacher Education." Unpublished doctoral diss., Michigan State University, East Lansing.

Ball, D.L., and G.W. McDiarmid. (1990). "The Subject-Matter Preparation of Teachers." In *Handbook of Research on Teacher Education* (pp. 437–449), edited by W.R. Houston. New York: Macmillan.

Barker, J.A. (1990). *The Power of Vision, Discovering the Future Series*. (Videotape). Burnsville, Minn.: Charthouse International Learning Corp.

Basseches, M. (1984). *Dialectical Thinking and Adult Development*. Norwood, N.J.: Ablex Publishing Corp.

Baumrind, D. (1971). "Current Patterns of Parental Authority." *Developmental Psychology Monograph* 4, 1, Pt. 2.

Baumrind, D. (1987). "A Developmental Perspective on Adolescent Risk Taking in Contemporary America." In *Adolescent Social Behavior and Health*, edited by C. Irwin, Jr. San Francisco: Jossey-Bass.

Beck, I. (1978). *An Analysis of Dimensions That Affect the Code Breaking Abilities in Eight Beginning Reading Programs*. Washington, D.C.: National Institute of Education. (ERIC 155-585).

Belenky, M.B., B.McV. Clinchy, N. Goldberger, and J.R. Tarule. (1986). *Women's Ways of Knowing: The Development of Self, Voice, and Mind*. New York: Basic Books.

Berreth, D., A. Crawford, A. Curran, and S. Nicklas. (1992). *Restructuring: Reflections of Practitioners*. Report of the 1992 ASCD Restructuring Forums. Alexandria, Va.: ASCD.

Brown, M.G. (1992). *Baldrige Award Winning Quality: How to Interpret the Malcolm Baldrige Criteria*, 2nd ed. Milwaukee, Wisc.: American Society for Quality Control Quality Press.

Bruner, J. (1962). *On Knowing: Essays for the Left Hand*. Cambridge, Mass.: Harvard University Press.

Buckman, J., and Z. Sharp-Burk. (1992). *The Partners for Quality Education Initiative Report*. St. Paul: Minnesota Academic Excellence Foundation.

Cohen, M. (1988). *Restructuring the Education System: Agenda for the 1990s.* Washington, D.C.: National Governors' Association.

Community Quality Coalition, World Center for Community Excellence, 1006 State St., Erie, PA 16501. Phone: (814) 456-9223.

Covey, S.R. (1989). *The Seven Habits of Highly Effective People.* New York: Simon and Schuster.

Darling-Hammond, L., and A.L. Goodwin. (1993). "Progress Toward Professionalism in Teaching." In *Challenges and Achievements of American Education,* edited by G. Cawelti. 1993 Yearbook of the Association for Supervision and Curriculum Development. Alexandria, Va.: ASCD.

Deci, E.L., and R.M. Ryan (1985). *Intrinsic Motivation and Self-Determination in Human Behavior.* New York: Plenum Press.

Deming, W.E. (1986). *Out of the Crisis.* Cambridge, Mass.: MIT Center for Advanced Engineering Study.

Deming, W.E. (June 2–5, 1992). *Leadership for the Transformation in the New Economic Age.* A Four-Day Intensive Seminar, St. Louis, Mo. [Manuscript submitted for publication].

Dweck, C.S. (1986). "Motivational Processes Affecting Learning." *American Psychologist* 41, 10: 1040–1048.

Doyle, W. (1986). "Classroom Organization and Management." In *Handbook of Research on Teaching* (pp. 392–431), edited by M.C. Wittrock. New York: Macmillan.

EPIE Institute. (1976). *National Study of the Nature and Quality of Instructional Materials: Materials Most Often Used by Teachers and Learners.* Report No. 76. Watermill, N.Y.: EPIE Institute.

Forrester, J. (June 12, 1991). "System Dynamics—Adding Structure and Relevance to Pre-College Education." *Pre-College Education* D-4227-1: 1–16. (Cambridge, Mass.: Massachusetts Institute of Technology; Phone: 617-253-1574).

Fullan, M.G. (1991). *The New Meaning of Educational Change.* New York: Teachers College Press.

Garvin, D.A. (November/December 1991). "How the Baldrige Award Really Works." *Harvard Business Review* 69, 6: 80–93.

Gilhool, T.F., F.J. Laski, and S.F. Gold. (1987). "A Legal Duty to Provide Effective Schooling." *Counterpoint* 8, 2: 4.

Glickman, C.D. (1986). "Developing Teacher Thought." *Journal of Staff Development* 7, 1: 6–21.

GOAL/QPC. (1989a). *The Memory Jogger: A Pocket Guide of Tools for Continuous Improvement.* Methuen, Mass.: GOAL/QPC. (Telephone: 508-685-3900).

GOAL/QPC. (1989b). *The Memory Jogger Plus+*[TM]*: Featuring the Seven Management and Planning Tools.* Methuen, Mass.: GOAL/QPC.

GOAL/QPC Research Committee. (1991). *Quality Function Deployment: Advanced QFD Application Articles.* 1990 Research Report. Methuen, Mass.: GOAL/QPC.

Goodlad, J.I. (1979). *What Schools Are For.* Bloomington, Ind.: Phi Delta Kappa Educational Foundation.

Goodlad, J.I. (1983). *A Place Called School.* New York: McGraw-Hill.

Goodlad, J.I. (1990). *Teachers For our Nation's Schools.* San Francisco: Jossey-Bass.

Goodman, K.S., P. Shannon, Y.S. Freeman, and S. Murphy. (1988). *Report Card on Basal Readers.* Katonah, N.Y.: Richard C. Owen Publishers.

Grossen, B., and D. Carnine. (1990). "Generalization and Transfer of Reasoning Skills." Unpublished manuscript.

Harvey, O.J. (Dec. 1970). "Beliefs and Behavior; Some Implications for Education." *Science Teacher* 37: 10–14.

Harvey, O.J., D.E. Hunt, and H.M. Schroder. (1961). *Conceptual Systems and Personality Organization.* New York: Wiley.

Hofmeister, A., S. Engelmann, and D. Carnine. (1989). "Developing and Validating Science Education Videodiscs." *Journal of Research in Science Teaching* 26: 665–677.

Jacobs, H.H., ed. (1989). *Interdisciplinary Curriculum: Design and Implementation.* Alexandria, Va.: ASCD.

Jenkins, J.R., M.L. Stein, and J.R. Osborn. (1981). "What Next After Decoding? Instruction and Research in Reading Comprehension." *Exceptional Education Quarterly* 2, 1: 27–40.

Joyce, B., with B. Showers. (1992). *Minnesota Business Partnership Education Quality Task Force Report from Academic Agenda Subcommittee.* Minneapolis: Minnesota Business Partnership.

Kearns, D.T. (April 20, 1988). "A Business Perspective on American Schooling." *Education Week* 32.

Kitchner, K.S. (1986). "The Reflective Judgment Model: Characteristics, Evidence, and Measurement." In *Adult Cognitive Development: Methods and Models* (pp.76–91), edited by R.A. Mines and K.S. Kitchner. New York: Praeger.

Liebman, M.S. (September 1992). "Getting Results from TQM." *Human Resource Magazine* 35–38.

Mathews, J., with P. Katel. (September 7, 1992). "Faced with Hard Times, Business Sours on Total Quality Management." *Newsweek* 48–49.

McCaslin, M., and T.L. Good. (1992). "Compliant Cognition: The Misalliance of Management and Instructional Goals in Current School Reform." *Educational Researcher* 21, 3: 4–16.

Minnesota Business Partnership. (March 1991). *An Education Agenda for Minnesota: The Challenge to Our Communities and Schools.* Minneapolis: Minnesota Business Partnership, IDS Center.

Minnesota Business Task Force. (December 1992). *Minnesota Business Partnership Education Quality Task Force Report from Academic Agenda Subcommittee.* Minneapolis: Minnesota Business Partnership.

Minnich, E.K. (1990). *Transforming Knowledge.* Philadelphia: Temple University Press.

Morehouse, R.E., R. Schenkat, and D. Battaglini. (1991). "Confidence in Content Through Conceptual Change." *Journal of Staff Development* 12, 2: 34–38.

Murphy, P.D., and M.M. Brown. (1970). "Conceptual Systems and Teaching Styles." *American Educational Research Journal* 7, 4: 529–540.

National Board of Professional Teaching Standards. (1991). *Toward High and Rigorous Standards for the Teaching Profession: Initial Policies and Perspectives of the National Board for Professional Teaching Standards.* 3rd ed. Washington, D.C.: Author.

Newman, J.H., Cardinal. (1973). *The Idea of a University.* Westminster, Md.: Christian Classics. [Originally published 1851].

Paris, S., T. Lawton, J. Turner, and J. Roth. (1991). "A Developmental Perspective on Standardized Achievement Testing." *Educational Researcher* 20, 5: 12–20.

Paul, R., A.J.A. Binker, K. Jensen, and H. Kreklau. (1987). *Critical Thinking Handbook: 4th–6th Grades: A Guide for Remodelling Lesson Plans in Language Arts, Social Studies, and Science.* Rohnert Park, Calif.: Sonoma State University's Center for Critical Thinking and Moral Critique.

Perkins, D. (1991). *Schools of Thought: The Necessary Shape of Education.* [Manuscript submitted for publication].

Perkins, D.N. (1992). "Classrooms: The Role of Distributed Intelligence." In *Smart Schools*, edited by D.N. Perkins. New York: Free Press.

Perry, W.G., Jr. (1981). "Cognitive and Ethical Growth: The Making of Meaning." In *Modern American College*, edited by A. Chickering. San Francisco: Jossey-Bass.

Persig, R.M. (1974). *Zen and the Art of Motorcycle Maintenance: An Inquiry into Values.* New York: Morrow.

Peters, T.J., and R.H. Waterman, Jr. (1982). *In Search of Excellence: Lessons from America's Best Run Companies.* New York: Harper and Row.

Pintrich, P.R. (1990). "Implications of Psychological Research on Student Learning and College Teaching for Teacher Education." In *Handbook of Research on Teacher Education* (pp. 826–857), edited by W.R. Houston. New York: Macmillan.

Reger, R. (1965, 1970). *School Psychology.* Springfield, Ill.: Charles C Thomas.

Reich, R. (1991a). "The Real Economy." *The Atlantic* 267, 2: 35–52.

Reich, R.B. (1991b). *The Work of Nations: Preparing Ourselves for 21st Century Capitalism.* New York: Random House.

Resnick, L., and D.P. Resnick. (1991). "Assessing the Thinking Curriculum Reform." In *Changing Assessments: Alternative View of Aptitude, Achievement, and Instruction*, edited by B.R. Gifford and M.C. O'Connor. Boston: Kluwer.

Roth, K. (April 1991). "Slow Nature of Conceptual Change in Disadvantaged Students." Paper presented at the annual meeting of the American Educational Research Association, Chicago.

Roth, K., K. Peasley, and C. Hazelwood. (1992). *Integration from the Student Perspective: Constructing Meaning in Science.* East Lansing: Michigan State University, Institute for Research on Teaching.

Sambs, C.E., and R. Schenkat. (May 1987). "Meeting Special Reading Needs in the Regular Classroom." *Counterpoint* 7, 2: 17.

Sambs, C.E., and R. Schenkat. (1990). "One District Learns About Restructuring." *Educational Leadership* 47, 7: 72–76.

Sarason, S.B. (1990). *The Predictable Failure of School Reform: Can We Change the Course Before It's Too Late?* San Francisco: Jossey-Bass.

Scardamalia, M., C. Bereiter, R.S. McLean, J. Swallow, and E. Woodruff. (1989). "Computer-Supported Intentional Learning Environments." *Journal of Educational Computing Research* 5, 1: 51–68.

Schenkat, R. (February 7, 1987). "A New View of Content and Student Evaluation." Paper presented at Eau Claire Area Reading Council, University of Wisconsin-Stout.

Schenkat, R. (November 16, 1988). "The Promise of Restructuring for Special Education." *Education Week* 36.

Schenkat, R.J., and D. Battaglini. (1980). "Special Education as a Great Experiment." *Education Unlimited* 5: 18–21.

Schenkat, R.J., D. Battaglini, and S.W. Rosen. (1985). *It Stands to Reason: The Rationale and Implementation of a Development-Based, Liberal Arts Oriented, Teacher-Education Program.* Reno, Nev.: Counterpoint Communications Company. (ED 263 059)

Schenkat, R., S. Sievers, and C. Goplen. (1991). "Beyond the Structure Imposed by Basal Reading Curriculum." Unpublished manuscript, Winona, Minn.: Public Schools.

Schenkat, R., and K. Tyser. (1986). "The Challenge of Teaching Higher Order Thinking Skills." *Journal of Staff Development* 7, 1: 22–34.

The Secretary's Commission on Achieving Necessary Skills. (1991). *What Work Requires of Schools: A SCANS Report for America 2000.* Washington, D.C.: U.S. Department of Labor.

Senge, P. (1990). *The Fifth Discipline: The Art and Practice of the Learning Organization.* New York: Doubleday.

Shannon, P. (1987). "Commercial Reading Materials: A Technological Ideology and the Deskilling of Teachers." *Elementary School Journal* 87, 3: 307–329.

Shulman, L. (1986). "Those Who Understand: Knowledge Growth in Teaching." *Educational Researcher* 15, 2: 4–14.

Shulman, L. (September 1987). "Assessment for Teaching: An Initiative for the Profession." *Phi Delta Kappan* 38–44.

Shulman, L. (April 1991). "Overcoming the 'Apprenticeship of Observation': Fostering Conceptual Change in the Teacher Education Classroom." Paper presented at the meeting of the American Educational Research Association, Chicago.

Slavin, R.E., and N.A. Madden. (February 1989). "What Works for Students at Risk: A Research Synthesis." *Educational Leadership* 46, 5: 4–13.

Smith. M. (1991). "Put to the Test: The Effects of External Testing on Teachers." *Educational Researcher* 20, 5: 8–11.

Spady, W.G., and K.J. Marshall. (1991). "Beyond Traditional Outcome-Based Education." *Educational Leadership* 49, 2: 67–72.

Stampen, J.O. (Winter 1987). "Improving the Quality of Education: W. Edwards Deming and Effective Schools." *Contemporary Education Review* 3, 3: 423–433.

Stayer, R. (November/December 1990). "How I Learned to Let My Workers Lead." *Harvard Business Review* 68, 6: 66–83.

Stevenson, H.W., and J.W. Stigler. (1992). *The Learning Gap: Why Our Schools Are Failing and What We Can Learn from Japanese and Chinese Education.* New York: Summit Books.

Stigler, J.W. (1987). "An Analysis of Addition and Subtraction Word Problems in U.S. and Soviet Elementary Mathematics Textbooks." Unpublished manuscript. Chicago: University of Chicago.

The Teacher Assessment Project. (1990). *Assessing the Teaching of Literacy in the Elementary Grades: Project Overview.* Technical Report No. L1. Stanford, Calif.: School of Education, Stanford University.

Toffler, A. (1990). *Powershift: Knowledge, Wealth, and Violence at the Edge of the 21st Century.* New York: Bantam Books.

Tyson Berstein, H., and A. Woodward. (1989). "Why Students Aren't Learning Very Much From Textbooks." *Educational Leadership* 47, 3: 14–17.

UAW/AMMO. (1991). "Making Quality Our Right." (Entire Issue). *UAW/AMMO* 27, 8: 1–23. (Detroit, Mich.: International Union, United Automobile, Aerospace and Agricultural Implement Workers of America).

Walton, M. (1986). *The Deming Management Method.* New York: Dodd, Mead.

Walton, M. (1991). *Deming Management at Work.* New York: Putnam.

Weick, K. (1976). "Educational Organizations as Loosely Coupled Systems." *Administrative Science Quarterly* 21: 1–19.

Wiggins, G. (November 1991). Personal Conversation at Assessment Conference. Bloomington, Minn.

Wilson, S.M., and S.S. Wineburg. (in press). "Wrinkles in Time and Place: Using Performance Assessment to Understand the Knowledge of History Teachers." *American Educational Research Journal.*

Wineburg, S.S. (1991). "On the Reading of Historical Texts: Notes on the Breach Between School and Academy." *American Educational Research Journal* 28: 495–519.

Wineburg, S.S., and S.M. Wilson. (1988). "Models of Wisdom in the Teaching of History." *Phi Delta Kappan* 70, 1: 50–58.

Woodward, A., and P. Komoski (1987). "The Imperative for Learner Verification and Revision." *Counterpoint* 8, 2: 4.

Woodward, G., and R. Schenkat. (August 1989). *An Investigation of Methods Used to Identify the Handicapped Learner.* Final Report of a Research Proposal, to the Minnesota Department of Education, Special Education Section. Winona, Minn.: Hiawatha Valley Special Education Cooperative, Winona Independent School District #861.

Zeichner, K., and B. Tabachnik. (1981). "Are the Effects of University Teacher Education Washed Out by School Experience?" *Journal of Teacher Education* 32, 3: 7–11.

Appendix A

"Best Practice" Related to Baldrige Criteria

This appendix lists the Malcolm Baldrige Award criteria, as shown in Figures 3.1 and 3.2, and expands on the educational applications of these criteria and of Total Quality Management (TQM), as expressed in the works of W. Edwards Deming. "Best practices" are those qualities of leadership, information analysis, and so forth—including changes in the core technologies of teaching and learning—that are needed for transformed schools today.

1.0 Leadership for Quality

Leadership practices allow teachers meaningful control over conditions of success:
- Scheduling (especially flexible correctives and enrichments).
- Time for growth.
- Teaching materials that staff believe support learning.
- Hiring, mentoring, and supporting teachers.

2.0 Information and Analysis

- Vision for the school site organized on a quality journey in a highly productive learning community, with professionals beyond the conventional image of teachers as solo performers. Staff work at a school site focused on continuous improvement by being organized to find and solve problems and locate, invent, and experiment with different methods of instruction and school organization.
- Skillful use of traditional and emerging assessments (such as portfolios, exhibitions) built from outcomes to track what students are learning—and not learning—and mindful of individuals, not averages. Encourage students to develop abilities in self-assessment.

3.0 Strategic Quality Planning

- Based on a vision of the interaction of all the educational implications of TQM and the Baldrige Criteria.

4.0 Human Resource Development and Management

• Demonstrate (and model for students) an open-ended capacity and commitment to lifelong professional development in a profession with many unsolved puzzles.

• Proficient teachers are models of educated persons exemplifying the virtues they seek to impart in students: careful reasoning, curiosity, love of learning, tolerance and openmindedness, fairness and justice, respect for human diversity and dignity. Teachers have the ability to take multiple perspectives, question received wisdom, be creative, take risks, and adopt a problem-solving and experimental orientation.

• Professionals have a content knowledge based on knowing how. Disciplinary thinking has developed rich, conceptual subject matter understandings; central concepts are organized; new knowledge is created; and perspectives and interpretations relate.

• Knowledge is seen as a combination of skills, dispositions, propositions, and beliefs that are integrated and flexible, elaborated, and deep—beyond reciting.

• Skilled in knowing analogies and illustrations to convey to students and know common conceptions students bring to learning situation; plus, a deep understanding of the students' communities and how their perspectives shape outlooks, values, and orientation.

• Skillful in traditional and emerging assessment (such as portfolios, exhibitions) built from outcomes, to track what students are learning—and not learning—and mindful of individuals, not averages. Encourage students to develop abilities in self-assessment.

• Familiar with concepts generated by social and cognitive scientists that apply to teaching and learning and employ motivation to build bridges with student interests. Encourage students to appreciate that often satisfaction of accomplishment comes from difficult work.

• Believe that all students can learn, accompanied by a belief in the dignity and worth of all.

5.0 Quality Assurance of Product and Service

Product

• Employ effectively and contextually a variety of generic teaching skills and materials, including use of technology and primary sources that support outcomes. Understand the legitimacy and limitations of diverse sources that inform teaching, and stay abreast of research in teaching and learning.

• Manage student groups by social norms that focus on learning, not merely control.

• Utilize human resources—tutors, aides, and volunteers, as well as complementary talents of peers.

• Quality time to plan.

• Technology-assisted management.

Forms of Schooling
• Reflects a continuum from current structures to schools as needed.
• Teachers in grades kindergarten through high school or in subject-matter areas determine the structure of classes.
• School day accommodating interdisciplinary programming.
• Mixed-age grouping.
• Student groups to accommodate individual interests for part of the day on school site.
• Develop student learning opportunities to accommodate learning within community.
• Students developing learning plans.
• The school site only used when it is the best facility to promote student's learning.

Process
• Vision for the school site organized on quality journey in a highly productive learning community, with professionals beyond the conventional image of teachers as solo performers. Staff members work at a school site focused on continuous improvement by being organized to find and solve problems and locate, invent, and experiment with different methods of instruction and school organization.
• Continually upgrading curriculum and instruction in a site-based context. Teachers who possess interpersonal skills work on teams to ensure a well-coordinated curriculum, thus assuring a continuity of learning experiences for children.
• Professional site embodies teachers who critically appraise commonplace school practices that may contradict emerging equity and excellence issues.
• Skills and understandings to avoid pitfalls and work to foster collaborative relationships between school and families, keeping in mind that the distinctive mission of teaching is to promote learning.
• Teachers work in a coordinated team with a variety of educational specialists.

6.0 Quality and Operational Results
• Relate to parents and constructively convey students' learning.

7.0 Customer Focus and Satisfaction
• Relate constructively to parents and convey student learnings and nonlearnings to them.
• Convey to students, parents, and the community the belief that all students can learn and the belief in the dignity and worth of all.

Appendix B

Graduation Outcomes:
High School Through Graduate School

Deriving educational outcomes of significance—what we want our students to know and be able to do—is an important step for schools on a quality journey. Because these outcomes are just as important for teachers and administrators as they are for students, we should examine expected outcomes at all levels of education. Educators at high school, community college, university, and graduate school levels contributed the following expected outcomes and presented them at a visitation day at Alverno College in Milwaukee in November 1990.

Wisconsin Education Association Council

- Learning to learn
- Listening ability
- Oral communications
- Problem solving
- Creative thinking
- Self-esteem
- Goal-setting
- Organizational effectiveness

Spalding University, Louisville, Kentucky

- Literacy skills
- Inquiry—critical thinking
- Numeracy
- Historical consciousness
- Scientific methodology
- Aesthetic and ethical values

Macomb Community College, Warren, Michigan

- Think critically
- Use communication skills effectively
- Be flexible and open to new ideas
- Increase understanding of self
- Understand and use quantitative information
- Have a worldwide perspective
- Recognize and assimilate interdisciplinary relationships
- Act and respond aesthetically
- Describe, evaluate, and effectively engage in social interactions

Purdue School of Pharmacy, Lafayette, Indiana

- Logical thinking and decision-making abilities
- Written communication abilities
- Oral communication abilities
- Effective listening and processing abilities
- Critical thinking abilities
- Evaluating and interpreting scientific and professional literature
- Self-learning abilities and habits
- Solving ethical problems
- Demonstrating leadership
- Adapting to a changing environment

University of Wisconsin-Madison, School of Medicine

- Analysis
- Appraisal
- Communications
- Interpersonal skills
- Self- and peer assessment
- Self-directed learning
- Handling of stress
- Completion of tasks
- Use of valuing and ethical considerations in decision making

National Curriculum Council of the United Kingdom

- Communication
- Problem solving

- Personal skills
- Numeracy
- Information technology
- Modern language competence

Appendix C

Proposed Standards of the National Board for Professional Teaching Standards

In an attempt to arrive at benchmarks of quality for teachers as professionals, the National Board for Professional Teaching Standards (NBPTS 1991) has published a description of proposed teaching standards. This appendix lists the five proposed standards, along with brief descriptive statements that appear in the document. For the full document, contact the NBPTS at the address listed on the next page.

Proposition 1: Teachers Are Committed to Students and Their Learning.

Teachers Recognize Individual Differences in Their Students and Adjust Their Practice Accordingly.

Teachers Have an Understanding of How Students Develop and Learn.

Teachers Treat Students Equitably.

Teachers' Mission Extends Beyond Developing the Cognitive Capacity of Their Students.

Proposition 2: Teachers Know the Subjects They Teach and How to Teach Those Subjects to Students.

Teachers Appreciate How Knowledge in Their Subjects Is Created, Organized, and Linked to Other Disciplines.

Teachers Command Specialized Knowledge of How to Convey a Subject to Students.

Teachers Generate Multiple Paths to Knowledge.

Proposition 3: Teachers Are Responsible for Managing and Monitoring Student Learning.

Teachers Call on Multiple Methods to Meet Their Goals.

Teachers Orchestrate Learning in Group Settings.

Teachers Place a Premium on Student Engagement.

Teachers Regularly Assess Student Progress.

Teachers Are Mindful of Their Principal Objectives.

Proposition 4: Teachers Think Systematically About Their Practice and Learn from Experience.

Teachers Are Continually Making Difficult Choices That Test Their Judgment.

Teachers Seek the Advice of Others and Draw on Education Research and Scholarship to Improve Their Practice.

Proposition 5: Teachers Are Members of Learning Communities.

Teachers Contribute to School Effectiveness by Collaborating with Other Professionals.

Teachers Work Collaboratively with Parents.

Teachers Take Advantage of Community Resources.

Source: National Board for Professional Teaching Standards. (1991). *Toward High and Rigorous Standards for the Teaching Profession: Initial Policies and Perspectives of the National Board for Professional Teaching Standards.* 3rd. ed. Washington, D.C.: Author.

For information contact:

Dr. Joan Baratz-Snowden
Vice President for Assessment and Research
National Board for Professional Teaching Standards
1320 18th St., N.W., Suite 401
Washington, DC 20036